HARK!

This Book Belongs to

Book 7

Content and Artwork by **Gooseberry Patch Company**

LEISURE ARTS
Vice President and Editor-in-Chief: Sandra Graham Case
Executive Director of Publications: Cheryl Nodine Gunnells
Director of Designer Relations: Debra Nettles
Senior Director of Publications: Susan White Sullivan
Publications Director: Kristine Anderson Mertes
Design Director: Cyndi Hansen
Special Projects Director: Susan Frantz Wiles
Art Operations Director: Jeff Curtis
Senior Director of Retail Marketing: Stephen Wilson

EDITORIAL STAFF
EDITORIAL
Senior Editorial Writer: Susan McManus Johnson
Contributing Editorial Writer: Suzie Puckett

TECHNICAL
Technical Editor: Leslie Schick Gorrell
Senior Technical Writer: Joyce Scott Harris
Technical Writer: Theresa Hicks Young

FOODS
Technical Assistant: Laura Siar Holyfield
Contributing Test Kitchen Staff: Rose Glass Klein

OXMOOR HOUSE
Editor-in Chief: Nancy Fitzpatrick Wyatt
Executive Editor: Susan Carlisle Payne
Foods Editors: Kelly Hooper Troiano
Assistant Foods Editor: McCharen Pratt
Photographers: Jim Bathie
Photo Stylists: Kay E. Clarke and Amy Wilson
Test Kitchens Director: Elizabeth Tyler Luckett
Test Kitchens Assistant Director: Julie Christopher
Test Kitchens Staff: Kristi Carter, Nicole Lee Faber, Kathleen Royal
  Phillips, Jan A. Smith, Elise Weiss and Kelley Self Wilton
Contributing Photographer: Brit Huckabay

DESIGN
Design Captain: Anne Pulliam Stocks
Designers: Cherece Athy, Tonya Bradford Bates, Polly Tullis Browning,
  Diana Sanders Cates, Kim Kern, Linda Diehl Tiano, Lori Wenger and
  Becky Werle

ART
Art Publications Director: Rhonda Hodge Shelby
Art Imaging Director: Mark Hawkins
Art Category Manager: Lora Puls
Lead Graphic Artist: Stephanie Hamling
Graphic Artists: Autumn Hall, Andrea Amerson Hazlewood,
  Stephanie Stephens and Dana Vaughn
Imaging Techicians: Steph Johnson and Mark R. Potter
Photo Stylists: Cassie Francioni and Karen Hall
Contributing Photo Stylists: Sondra Daniel, Christy Myers
  and Jan Nobles
Photographer: Lloyd Litsey
Publishing Systems Administrator: Becky Riddle
Publishing Systems Assistants: Clint Hanson, Josh Hyatt
  and John Rose

BUSINESS STAFF
Vice President and Chief Operations Officer: Tom Siebenmorgen
Director of Corporate Planning and Development:
  Laticia Mull Dittrich
Vice President, Sales and Marketing: Pam Stebbins
Director, National Accounts: Martha Adams
Director of Sales and Services: Margaret Reinold
Vice President, Operations: Jim Dittrich
Comptroller, Operations: Rob Thieme
Retail Customer Service Manager: Stan Raynor
Print Production Manager: Fred F. Pruss

Copyright © 2005 by Gooseberry Patch, 600 London, Delaware, Ohio 43015,
www.gooseberrypatch.com (illustrations, recipes and crafts). Copyright © 2005 by
Leisure Arts, Inc., 5701 Ranch Drive, Little Rock, Arkansas 72223-9633,
www.leisurearts.com (layout, photography, crafts and recipes). All rights reserved. This
publication is protected under federal copyright laws. Reproduction of this publication or
any other Leisure Arts publication, including publications which are out of print, is
prohibited unless specifically authorized. This includes, but is not limited to, any form of
reproduction or distribution on or through the Internet, including posting, scanning or e-
mail transmission. We have made every effort to ensure that these recipes and instructions
are accurate and complete. We cannot, however, be responsible for human error,
typographical mistakes or variations in individual work. Made in the United States of America.

Library of Congress Catalog Number 99-71586
Hardcover ISBN 1-57486-364-9
Softcover ISBN 1-57486-365-7

10 9 8 7 6 5 4 3 2 1

Gooseberry Patch Christmas

Book 7

A LEISURE ARTS PUBLICATION

Gooseberry Patch

Christmas

Gooseberry Patch

This is for all our friends who can't resist the urge to make snow angels and then toast their tootsies by a crackling fire...happy holidays!

How Did Gooseberry Patch Get Started?

You may know the story of Gooseberry Patch...the tale of two country friends who decided one day over the backyard fence to try their hands at the mail order business. Started in Jo Ann's kitchen back in 1984, Vickie & Jo Ann's dream of a "Country Store in Your Mailbox" has grown and grown to a 96-page catalog with over 400 products, including cookie cutters, Santas, snowmen, gift baskets, angels and our very own line of cookbooks! What an adventure for two country friends!

Through our catalogs and books, Gooseberry Patch has met country friends from all over the world. While sharing letters and phone calls, we found that our friends love to cook, decorate, garden and craft. We've created Kate, Holly & Mary Elizabeth to represent these devoted friends who live and love the country lifestyle the way we do. They're just like you & me... they're our "Country Friends®!"

Your friends at Gooseberry Patch

Mary Elizabeth * Holly * Kate * Spot

Table of Contents

Keeping Christmas

Home for Christmas

Keeping CHRISTMAS

This year, do something truly special with your holiday photos and greeting cards...use them to make a Christmas calendar, a festive family tree and other fun mementos. You'll have a wonderful time displaying all your favorite memories. And any of these heartwarming creations would also make thoughtful gifts!

Celebrate Christmas with a scrapbook-style Family Calendar. Once it's completed, you can make copies to share with everyone on your gift list. Turn to page 120 to learn how easy it is to preserve your magical holiday memories.

Dear Santa,

Pleas bring me a puppy.

And toys for my

bruther. Love, Alex

dear Santa

★ The night before Christmas ★

DECEMBER

S	M	T	W	T	F	S

Home for the Holidays

Holiday Wishes

4	5	6	7	1	2	3
11	12	13	14	8	9	10
18	19	20	21	15	16	17
25	26	27	28	22	23	24
			29	30		31

'Tis the Season

Make It Merry

F W

The brightest ornaments on this Christmas tree will be the smiling faces of your loved ones! Your favorite snapshots get festive with scrapbook supplies and a minimum of work. How-to's for the Family Photo Tree are on page 120.

Christmas memories are some of the sweetest and fondest of those we carry through our lives. From our earliest childhood recollection, Christmas memories are stored in a special place in our hearts, to be recalled during quiet times of reminiscing. My family grew up in Pennsylvania where we enjoyed many Christmases together. In 1969, my parents secretly taped all four children opening presents as Dad pulled each gift from under the tree. Later that day, we added our own commentary to the celebration tape. Each Christmas thereafter, we gather to listen to and relive that special Christmas. Dad has since passed away, which makes the tape all the more precious and cherished. I hope to continue the tradition with our three children this Christmas.

—Cyndy Rogers
Upton, MA

A simple box of photos taken through the years makes the very best "coffee table" conversation starter.

Have you ever sent out all your greeting cards, only to discover that you've forgotten someone? Make your Christmas correspondence easier by converting an ordinary box into a Card Organizer. It will hold all the cards you receive this year, along with their envelopes. When you get ready to address next year's cards, you'll have all the information you need in one place. The instructions for this quick and memorable fix are on page 121.

God has given us our memories, that we might have roses in December.

—J.M. BARRIE—

Christmas is for the child in all of us, so who better to decorate this year's greeting cards than little ones? Get the kids busy on their merry masterpieces, then turn to page 121 to create the cheeriest greetings ever made!

A homemade checkerboard that will bring smiles, win or lose... decoupage a grandchild's picture over every other square of a pre-painted checkerboard. Copy and reduce photos, if necessary, on a color photocopier.

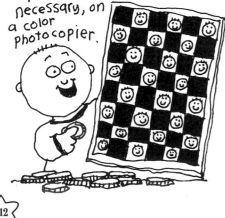

My favorite Christmas memory is putting up a small fireplace that was made of cardboard. We lived in a small house and Mom would make hot cocoa for my sister and me while we worked. We would then hang our stockings on our fireplace with shiny tacks. We would color in front of that lighted fireplace, sing carols and tell each other stories!

—Michelle Bagby
Templeton, CA

When my dad was a child in the 1940's, he and his siblings would write down their lists of wishes for Santa Claus on pieces of paper. They would then tear up the lists, sprinkle the pieces in the fireplace, then run outside quickly and watch as the smoke rose from the chimney, magically sending their Christmas lists on the way to Santa. This memory always makes me smile.

—Patricia Van Wyk
Newton, IA

I don't need to be rich; my children are my treasures.
⟡ MYRNA JEAN JOHNSON ⟡

Start a new tradition that involves everyone in your family! Kids big and little can add drawings, notes, photos and memories to your Christmas Journal. It's fun to see the pages fill up with sweet memories and fun stories. The easy instructions are on page 121.

remember all those toys baby loved?

Each year, my nieces and nephews come to decorate my Christmas tree. They each have to bring one homemade ornament and I make each of them an ornament. They each have a box that their ornaments go in. Every year, as we open the boxes, we fondly remember when they made this or that ornament. Soon we are traveling down memory lane 'til the last memory is hung. When they grow older and are on their own, I will give them their boxes for their own trees.

—Rita Wood
East Sparta, OH

Memory is the treasury and guardian of all things.
@ -MARCUS TULLIUS CICERO-

What a cheerful way to remember Christmases past! A Memory Shadow Box displays your holiday trinkets in a clever way. Use ornaments, photos, tags, cards…whatever you'd like! You'll find the instructions on page 122.

14

Is there someone you would especially like to remember at Christmas this year? Create a Memory Wreath! A loved one will be delighted to see their own photo tucked into the greenery along with holiday ornaments, mementos and ribbon. Learn how to make this very special decoration on page 122.

Among my treasures, I have a brooch that belonged to my Grandma. It is shaped like a Christmas tree and has multicolored rhinestones set in its branches. Grandma liked to wear that brooch every Christmas. She wore it to church, while she made the holiday dinner and even when playing with her rowdy great-grandchildren. And as much as that little tree sparkled, Grandma's smile was still brighter. My dear Grandma left us last year at Christmas. At the time, I couldn't imagine the holidays ever being happy again. But now I realize that she will spend every Christmas with the One whose birthdays she loved to celebrate. This year, I think I will wear Grandma's little Christmas tree brooch in her honor. It will be a sweet reminder of her beautiful smile.

—Susan Johnson
Little Rock, AR

♥ I remember my annual CHRISTMAS SHOPPING TRIP with GRANDMA

W hat's your favorite memory of Christmas?
Is it a tree filled with heartfelt, handmade
ornaments? Or a stack of gifts wrapped in vintage
linens? Maybe it's greeting cards lined up to wish you
holiday cheer? If you ask Mary Elizabeth, Holly, and
Kate, you'll get three different answers, but the
Gooseberry Patch friends all agree on one thing:
There's nothing like filling your house with Christmas
decorations to make you feel like a kid again!

*Add a bit of whimsy this year…whip up a
Latch-Hooked Rug and a Latch-Hooked Wreath
with big, fluffy snowballs all over. Turn to pages
122 and 123 to learn how fleece fabric makes
these holly-jolly decorations so much fun!*

A Vintage Touch

Keeping Christmas is a tradition that comes from the heart. And since the Country Friends all have memories of their Grandmothers' pretty cotton handkerchiefs, they think this sweet holiday theme is extra-special. Now, no one wants to cut up Grandma's hankies, so it's probably best to use flea market or reproduction ones. You'll get the same lovely, vintage look, either way.

Holly's Hankie Garland

Here's a fast and easy decoration that will catch everyone's attention!

Make your garland as long as you like... make 2, make 3... it's easy as can be.

Simply cut 4 triangles from your hankie (figure one), or if your hankie is smaller, cut 2 triangles (figure two).

FIG. ONE

FIG. TWO

Sew or glue the raw edges of your triangles to a length of ribbon. Attach buttons at the corners and you're ready to decorate!

Sweet nostalgia makes these lovely ornaments even more beautiful. They're destined to become family heirlooms.

FRAMED HANKIE ORNAMENTS

Make your vintage handkerchiefs the focal point of your tree by framing them. Purchase wooden frames in various shapes and sizes and paint them cream. Remove the mats from the frames and cover with fabric. Cut a corner from a hanky and glue it to the mat or edge of the frame; you could even position a hankie to be a pocket! Adorn with decorative ribbons, rick-rack, tags, charms or buttons. On one of the frames, you may want to include a treasured photograph along with a decorated tag documenting the occasion. For hangers, glue the ends of a length of ribbon to the back of each frame.

VINTAGE PILLOW ORNAMENTS

Don't toss handkerchiefs that have a little wear! Cut a square from the usable portion (center the design if possible) and turn them into keepsakes for the tree! Start by cutting the hankie to the desired size. Cut a piece of backing fabric the same size. Sew rick-rack along edges of backing fabric. With right sides together and leaving an opening for turning, sew hankie piece and backing together. Turn right side out; stuff with polyester fiberfill and sew the opening closed. For hanger, cut a length of trim and tack ends to center top of ornament. Use fabric glue to embellish as desired with buttons, ribbons and trims.

This distinctive Nine Point Tree Skirt is a charming foundation for your tree. Turn to page 124 for instructions to fashion this timeless beauty.

HANKIE TUSSY MUSSIES

A tussy mussy is a dainty bouquet holder made from fabric or lace and filled with sweet-smelling flowers or herbs. These fragrant bouquets were carried by ladies of the Victorian era wherever they went. A lady would place the flowers a gentleman sent her in her tussy mussy to show she reciprocated his feelings.

To make your tussy mussy, fold a hankie in half twice. Fold opposite corners in and sew the two sides together to form a cone. Adorn the edges of the tussy mussy with rick-rack, ribbons, and buttons. Add a ribbon hanger to proudly display your tussy mussy on the Christmas tree or door handle or even on the wall as a sconce. Fill with fresh greenery and berries or flowers from your special someone!

HANDKERCHIEF MANTEL SCARF

Add sentimental warmth to your mantel for the holidays by transforming vintage handkerchiefs into a mantel scarf. Measure the depth (including 3" for drop length) and length of your mantel; add 1" for seam allowances. Cut a piece of fabric this size for scarf. Press one long edge and ends of scarf ¼" to wrong side. Press ¼" to wrong side again, then topstitch to secure. Cut hankies in half diagonally. Cut triangles of white cotton fabric 1¼" larger than hankie triangles. Use fusible web tape to fuse short sides of each white triangle ¼" to wrong side. Sew lengths of red rick-rack ½" from short edges of white triangles. Pin hankies ½" from edges of rick-rack and trim long edge of white triangle even with long edge of hankie triangle. Overlapping triangles to fit and matching right sides and raw edges, sew triangles to scarf; turn to right side and press.

The first time I went to a department store as a child and saw a Christmas tree, I wanted a tree as beautiful as the one I'd seen. Everything was perfect...matching bows and huge glass ball ornaments all perfectly arranged on the tree. Now, as a wife and mother, I have the perfect tree each year. It's decorated with cowboys, dolls and ornaments made in school...ones given to my children with their names on them. Even fishing bobbers adorn my tree. Each year, as my children decorate the tree with their beloved ornaments, I often think that we do have the most beautiful tree... a tree decorated with love, family and ornaments made from the heart.

—Angie Venable
Gooseberry Patch

Memories are not the key to the past, but to the future. ~ CORRIE ten BOOM

FRAMED HANKIE CARD HOLDER

- cream wooden frame with a 23¹/₂"x12¹/₂" opening
- 24"x12" piece of foam core board
- ¹/₂ yd. red and white striped fabric
- ¹/₂ yd. green fabric
- red rick-rack and trim
- ¹/₄"w mini red check ribbon
- dimensional foam dots
- assorted red buttons
- craft knife
- Christmas charms
- vintage hankies
- ³/₄" brass fasteners
- alphabet tags
- craft glue

1. For covered board, cut a piece of foam core board to fit frame. Cover foam core with striped fabric.

2. Cut a 36"x20" piece of green fabric. Fold fabric in half lengthwise.

3. With fold of fabric at top, overlap fabric 1" over sides and bottom of foam core. Glue sides in place. Making pockets 8" wide, create pockets with ¹/₂"w pleats (Fig. 1); glue overlap at bottom to back of foam core. Cut small holes through fabric and foam core ¹/₄" from top and bottom of each pleat. Insert a brass fastener to secure pleat.

4. Cut hankies in half diagonally and fold over top of each pocket; tack to back of pocket top. Sew a charm to point of each hankie.

5. Insert covered board into frame. String alphabet tags onto a length of trim to spell "Merry Christmas!" Use foam dots to hold the trim ends to the frame.

6. Glue a button to each fastener and foam dot, then finish with rick-rack, ribbon, and buttons.

Fig. 1

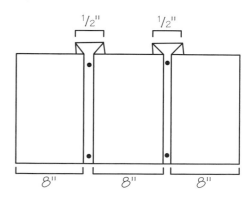

HANKIE WALL HANGING

- vintage handkerchiefs
- 1½ yds striped fabric
- 27½" square of background fabric
- red buttons
- 2½ yds red rick-rack
- assorted beads, bells and snaps
- fabric, ribbon and trim scraps
- embroidery floss
- batting
- hanging rod

Match right sides and use a ¼" seam allowance for all sewing unless otherwise indicated.

1. Leaving a 3¼" border on all sides and positioning one hankie for the pocket, arrange hankies on background fabric, overlapping as desired and pin in place. Sew hankies in place then sew a rick-rack border ½" from edges of hankies.

2. For fabric border, cut two 3¼"x27½" side strips and two 33½"x3¼" top/bottom strips from striped fabric. Sew side strips, then top and bottom strips to decorated background piece. Embellish as desired with folded hankies, trims, tags and buttons.

3. Cut one 33½" square of striped fabric for backing and a 3"x32" piece of striped fabric for hanging sleeve. Press ends, then edges of hanging sleeve ½" to wrong side. Center sleeve on backing 1" from top edge. Sew long edges in place, leaving ends open for the hanging rod.

4. Cut one 33½" square of batting. Place top piece and backing right sides together. Lay both pieces on top of batting and pin all three layers together. Leaving an opening for turning, sew along edges of wall hanging. Turn right side out and sew opening closed. Topstitch ¼" from edges of wall hanging. Sew layers together along seam of background fabric and borders and along edges of hankies.

There are few holidays that Mom doesn't include someone who would otherwise be alone. She always takes on the responsibility to make sure everyone has a happy day filled with love. Of course, growing up, we didn't realize all she did until we were grown with families of our own. Today, with four generations, she still manages to make each of us feel special and loved…our holidays are filled with joy and togetherness.

— Elena Tonkin
Powell, TN

Jingle · Jingle · Jingle!

Thread jingle bells on a cord or string, knot the ends together, and hang on the knob of your front door. What a merry sound for arriving guests to hear!

Merrily monogrammed

Personalize a stocking for every member of your family with these quick & easy stockings that everyone is sure to love!

CROSS STITCHED MONOGRAM CHRISTMAS STOCKING

Using the stocking pattern on page 140, follow *Making Patterns*, page 134, to trace the stocking pattern onto tracing paper. Use the pattern to cut 2 stocking pieces from wool and 2 lining pieces from print fabric. Matching right sides, using a ½-inch seam allowance and leaving the top open, sew stocking pieces together; turn right side out. Repeat to sew lining pieces together; do not turn right side out.

For cuff, cut a 3½"x15" strip of 18 ct linen. Also cut a 1½"x15" strip and a 5½"x15" strip of print fabric. Matching long edges, sew 1½"w strip to top and 5½" strip to bottom of linen. Referring to *Cross Stitch*, page 136, and the alphabet, page 141, center and cross stitch monogram on linen. Matching sides and long edges; press. Matching right sides sew ends of cuff together to form a ring. Matching wrong sides and raw edges, fold bottom of print fabric up into cuff.

Matching raw edges, place lining in stocking. Matching top edges and centering cuff seam at back, place cuff in lining. For the hanger, matching right sides and long edges, fold a 1½"x5" piece of print fabric in half; sew together along long edges. Turn right side out; press. Place the hanger between the cuff and stocking at heel-side seam. Sew pieces together along the top edges. Fold cuff to the outside.

*Oh, what fun to decorate your window with Cross Stitched Monogram Ornaments!
You'll find the instructions for these letter-perfect pretties on page 125.*

Those gifts are ever the most acceptable which the giver makes precious.

— OVID —

Beaded Monogram

Add some sparkle to your tree with beaded monogram ornaments. Simply print out a letter on your home computer and enlarge it to the desired size. Use the printed letter as a guide to bend a length of 20-gauge wire into the shape of the letter. Depending on the letter, you may have to use more than one piece of wire. Make a small eye loop at one end of the wire, thread beads onto the wire, then make a small eye loop at the remaining end to secure the beads in place. Repeat for additional beaded wire to complete the letter; twist beaded wires together at intersections to join them. Add a ribbon hanger to top of the beaded letter.

Make a sparkling gift in no time. It's as simple as threading beads onto wire, but oh-so dazzling! Beaded Monograms are wonderful ornaments for the tree, but Holly also likes to use them on gifts and wreaths.

Personalize a pillow. . .chenille yarn is stitched needlepoint-style on a purchased latch hook canvas pillow cover. Turn to page 125 for the instructions .

MONOGRAMMED HAND TOWEL

Turn a plain white cloth napkin into a vintage looking hand towel by adding a few simple details. Begin by sewing a length of crocheted lace along one edge of the napkin. Then cut a 2" wide strip of vintage fabric and press the raw edges ¼" to the wrong side. Topstitch the strip 1" from the edge of the napkin. Trace the desired monogram, page 141, onto tissue paper. Pin tissue paper in place above the fabric strip. Stitching through tissue paper, embroider letter using 3 strands of embroidery floss for *Satin Stitch* and 2 strands for *Backstitch*, pages 136-137. Carefully tear away tissue paper when embroidery is complete. Sew a rick-rack border around the monogram. Embellish with additional rick-rack and assorted vintage buttons.

A Monogrammed Tissue Box Cover brings holly-jolly cheer to the powder room. See page 125 to make this quick & easy tissue box cover.

Surprise an overnight holiday guest with her own pretty monogrammed hand towel in the bathroom!

Warm & Woolly

*If ever there's a fabric that looks as cozy as it feels,
it's good old-fashioned wool. These days, you can find hand-dyed wool
in a rainbow of colors. The rustic texture is reminiscent of country cabins and
a comfy evening by the fire. What a great way to make your Christmas décor…
and your Christmas gifts…as heartwarming as you could wish!*

I make the most
of all that comes
and the least of all that goes. — Sara Teasdale

The recipe for happy feet is a warm ottoman cover accented with wool appliqué! Once the Country Friends started creating these fancy footrest covers, they just couldn't stop until they finished three inviting designs (see pages 128 & 129). And can you guess the easy secret to shaping these wonderful wool trees? You can read all about it on pages 126-127.

Take your needle, my child, and work at your pattern; it will come out like a rose by and by. Life is like that; one stitch at a time taken *patiently*, and the pattern will come out all right, like embroidery.
— Oliver Wendall Holmes

With its button berries, star appliqués and simple embroidery, the Stitched Wall Hanging reminds us that the best gifts come from the heart.

STITCHED WALL HANGING

- $1/2$ yard of green hand-dyed wool
- $1/3$ yard of oatmeal hand-dyed wool
- scraps of red and dark gold hand-dyed wool
- $1/2$ yard red check homespun fabric
- $1/4$" and $3/4$" dia. red buttons
- $1/4$" dia. green shank buttons
- $1/2$ yard of $1/4$"w variegated green silk ribbon
- gold, green, and red embroidery floss
- $3/4$"w gold grosgrain ribbon
- 17" length of $1/2$" dia. dowel rod
- two $1 1/4$"dia. wooden balls
- tissue paper
- pinking shears

Refer to Embroidery Stitches, pages 136-137, before beginning project. Use 2 strands of floss for all stitching unless otherwise indicated.

For wall hanging front, cut a 14"x11" piece of oatmeal felt. Trace verse, page 145, onto tissue paper. Center and pin verse on oatmeal felt piece. Stitching through tissue paper and using green floss, work Back Stitches and French Knots over words. Carefully tear away tissue paper. For pine branches, cut silk ribbon in half; fold ribbon in half lengthwise and tack in place along each side of verse. Work gold floss Straight Stitches along silk ribbon to create pine needles. Cut assorted size "berries" from red felt. Work Straight Stitches to attach felt berries along pine branches, then sew $1/4$" red buttons for "berries" along branches.

Trace star patterns, page 145, onto tissue paper. Using patterns, cut 3 stars from gold felt. Work gold Blanket Stitches along edges of stars to attach stars to front piece. For green backing, cut a $15 1/2$"x$12 1/2$" piece of green felt. Work red Blanket Stitches to attach front piece to green backing. Cut scallops along edges of green backing. Work gold Blanket Stitches along edges of border scallops. Sew green buttons along scallops. Tear a $16 1/2$"x13" piece of homespun. Tack decorated felt piece to homespun. For hanging tabs, use pinking shears to cut three $1 1/4$"x6" strips of green felt. Cut three 6" lengths of grosgrain ribbon. Work long red Running Stitches to attach ribbons to felt strips. Folding hangers in half, pin hangers evenly along top edge of wall hanging. Sew a red button through all layers. Insert dowel rod through hangers. Secure a wooden ball at each end of dowel rod.

30

EMBROIDERED TOTE BAG

Think of all the shopping you can do with this handy tote bag to help hold all your packages!

Match right sides and use a 1/2" seam allowance for all sewing unless otherwise indicated.

For front and back of bag, cut two 18¹⁄₂"x10¹⁄₂" pieces of burgundy wool. For bottom of bag, cut one 9¹⁄₄"x11¹⁄₂" piece of burgundy wool. For borders, cut two 18¹⁄₂"x3¹⁄₄" pieces of cream wool. Sew cream wool along bottoms of front and back pieces. With wrong sides together, sew short edges of front and back pieces together. With the side seams centered at each short edge of bottom piece and matching wrong sides, sew the bottom to the bag. Work green Blanket Stitches along top and bottom edges of borders and down side seams.

For the handles, cut two 2"x 34" strips of cream wool. Fold strips in half lengthwise; topstitch along raw edges. Sew ends of one strip 5" from each side of front of tote. Repeat for remaining strip on back of tote.

Trace patterns, page 144, onto tissue paper. Using patterns, cut appliqués from wool. Refer to photo and work Blanket Stitches to secure appliqués on front of bag.

For lining, cut one 9¹⁄₄"x11¹⁄₂" and two 18¹⁄₂"x10¹⁄₂" pieces of cotton fabric. With right sides together, sew short edges of front and back pieces together. With the side seams centered at each short edge of bottom piece and matching right sides, sew the bottom to the lining. Turn top edge of lining under ¹⁄₄" and press. Insert lining in tote bag and sew together along top edge.

Whether used as a handbag or to enclose a gift, this beautiful bag is meant to hold wonderful things! The Dyed Wool & Embroidery Drawstring Bag is as practical as it is pretty… its gathered closure keeps its contents secure, while the flat bottom helps it to stand upright. You'll find the instructions on page 128.

Print holiday sentiments on vellum using old-fashioned curly fonts for heartfelt wishes. Punch out the message using circular or square hand-held paper punches. Attach to packages with cotton string.

Comforts of Home

This Christmas, decorate with vintage accessories. You'll have a jolly time shopping at flea markets and resale shops for just the right pieces. Cheery red & white decorations deliver an extra measure of holiday joy.

FOUR-PATCH ORNAMENT

Cut squares from assorted tea towels and coordinating fabrics to make one of these ornaments. Sew four 3" squares together; baste crocheted lace along the edges. Cut a 10" length of twill tape for the hanger; matching ends and raw edges, baste ends to one edge of ornament front. Tack a crocheted doily and crocheted trim to center front of ornament. For backing, cut a 6" square from a tea towel or coordinating fabric. Matching right sides and leaving an opening at bottom for turning, sew ornament front to ornament back. Clip the seam allowance at the corners. Turn ornament right side out. Slipstitch opening closed.

Search out vintage fabrics in splashy vegetable prints, then make color photocopies. Cut out squares and attach to the front of a small brown paper bag using spray adhesive. Set a jar of relish inside, turn down bag edges and tie on a gift tag...so easy!

"What is Christmas? It is tenderness for the past, courage for the present, hope for the future. It is a fervent wish that every cup may overflow with blessings rich and eternal, and that every path may lead to peace."
— Agnes M. Pharo

Tag sale or flea market finds are perfect for giving your tree a vintage look. The four-patch ornament was made from a variety of tea towels found at a flea market.

Collectibles, such as this cute, crocheted dress, give a sweet, old-fashioned charm to your tree.

Shopping is a woman thing. It's a contact sport like football. Women enjoy the scrimmage, the noisy crowds, the danger of being trampled to death, and the ecstasy of the purchase.

-ERMA BOMBECK-

FLEA

TEA TOWEL TREE SKIRT

For a nostalgic holiday feel, create a clever tree skirt from vintage tea towels. If your towels aren't the same size, trim and hem them to match.

- six 18"x27" tea towels (cut and hemmed to size if necessary)
- four 10" squares of fabric for center
- six 4¹/₂" squares of fabric for points
- crocheted trim

Use a ¹/₂" seam allowance.

1. For center, press one corner of each 10" square 2" to wrong side. With wrong sides and pressed edges facing, refer to Fig. 1 to sew three sides of squares together; hem remaining two sides and pressed corners.

2. Overlapping towels and aligning inner edges according to Fig. 2, arrange tea towels over center; leaving one towel's edges open as indicated, pin towels in place.

3. Place 4¹/₂" fabric squares under towels to complete points; press outer edges to wrong side, then pin in place.

4. Leaving the designated opening unsewn, sew along the inner edges of the towels and triangles to join pieces together; hem edges of opening. Trim seam allowances as needed.

5. Pin, then sew crocheted trim along outside edges of tree skirt, adjusting trim as needed.

6. Hand sew decorative stitches along inner edges of towels (we chose a herringbone stitch, see Embroidery, pages 136-137).

Fig. 1

Fig. 2

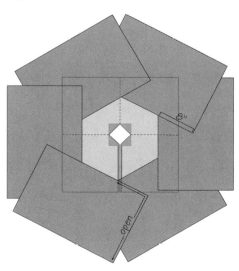

CROCHET CENTER PILLOW

A vintage tablecloth and crocheted potholders found at the flea market can be combined to make fantastic pillows for your home. Cut two 17" squares from the tablecloth. Baste crocheted lace to edges of pillow front. Tack crocheted potholder to center of pillow. Matching right sides and leaving an opening for turning, sew pillow front to pillow back. Clip the seam allowance at the corners. Turn pillow right side out; insert pillow form. Slipstitch opening closed.

A good conscience is a continual Christmas.
— BENJAMIN FRANKLIN —

QUILT

Yardage is based on 43"/44" wide fabric with a "usable" width of 40" after shrinkage and trimming selvages. Use a $1/4$" seam allowance.

- $3/4$ yard each of six assorted fabrics
- $4 1/8$ yards of backing fabric
- $1/2$ yard of fabric for binding
- twin-size batting trimmed to 60" x 73"

Cut a total of eighty 7" squares from assorted fabrics. Sew 8 squares together to make a row. Sew 10 rows together to make quilt top.

To piece backing, cut backing fabric into two lengths. Place lengths with right sides facing and sew long edges together, forming a tube. Match seams and press along one fold. Cut along pressed fold to form single piece.

(continued on page 129)

A welcome spot of color on a winter day, this cozy quilt looks so inviting! You're sure to want to snuggle up and sit for a spell.

CRANBERRY-ALMOND BLONDIES

$1/2$ c. butter, softened
16-oz. pkg. brown sugar
3 eggs
1 T. vanilla extract
2 c. self-rising flour
$1^{1}/2$ c. slivered almonds, toasted
    and divided
1 c. dried cranberries
Powdered sugar, for dusting

Preheat oven to 350 degrees. Beat butter and brown sugar together at medium speed with a mixer. Add eggs and vanilla until blended. Gradually add flour until blended. Fold $^{3}/4$ cup almonds into batter. Spoon batter into a greased and floured 13"x9" baking pan. Sprinkle cranberries and remaining almonds over top of batter. Bake for 20 minutes; reduce temperature to 325 and bake 25 more minutes. Cool in pan on a wire rack. Dust with powdered sugar and cut into squares. Makes 16 servings.

TEA TOWEL GIFT BAGS

Transform vintage tea towels of your grandmother's into unique gift bags for the family. Simply fold a tea towel in half with right sides facing, then sew up the sides. Turn the bag right side out. Add some crocheted trim around the top edges and use a length of twill tape for the tie. Add your gift and you're done!

If you're looking for a sweet treat to make for the office Christmas party or church social, these Cranberry-Almond Blondies are just the thing! We used a vintage doily, picked up at the local flea market, to add a festive holiday look.

"Christmas in Bethlehem. The ancient dream: a cold, clear night made brilliant by a glorious star, the smell of incense, shepherds and wise men falling to their knees in adoration of the sweet baby, the incarnation of perfect love."
— Lucinda Franks

The GREAT Disappearing Snack Mix!

THIS RED & WHITE MIX IS PERFECT TO TUCK INTO TEA TOWEL GIFT BAGS WITH PLENTY LEFT OVER TO SNACK ON!

12·OZ. PKG. CHOCOLATE CHIPS
16·OZ. PKG. SALTED PEANUTS
11·OZ. PKG. SESAME STICKS
12·OZ. PKG. WHITE CHOCOLATE CHIPS
12·OZ. PKG. VANILLA YOGURT-COVERED RAISINS
2 6·OZ. PKGS. DRIED CRANBERRIES
10·OZ. CAN CASHEWS

MIX ALL INGREDIENTS TOGETHER IN A LARGE MIXING BOWL. STORE IN PLASTIC ZIPPING BAGS. MAKES 4 QUARTS.

A YUMMY RECIPE FROM KRISTINE MERTES ★ LITTLE ROCK, AR

These reusable goodie bags will bring as many smiles as the treats packed inside! Fashioned from cheery red & white fabric, the gift sacks are sure to be used year round.

CHRISTMAS
with all the trimmings

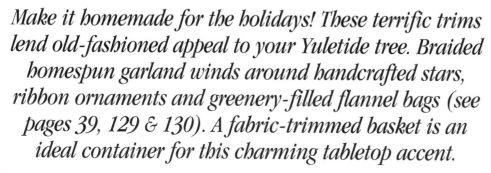

Make it homemade for the holidays! These terrific trims lend old-fashioned appeal to your Yuletide tree. Braided homespun garland winds around handcrafted stars, ribbon ornaments and greenery-filled flannel bags (see pages 39, 129 & 130). A fabric-trimmed basket is an ideal container for this charming tabletop accent.

FLANNEL BAG ORNAMENT

Trace the flannel bag pattern from page 146 onto tracing paper; cut out. Use the pattern to cut 2 bag pieces from flannel. Matching right sides, using a 1/2" seam allowance and leaving the top open, sew flannel pieces together; turn right side out. Press top edge of bag 1/4" to inside; topstitch in place. Cut one 18" length and two 6 1/2" lengths of 3/8" wide ribbon. Referring to Fig. 1 and taping ends down, lay 6 1/2" lengths of ribbon flat on a table; weave 18" ribbon through 6 1/2" lengths. Wrap woven ribbons around bag; stitch ribbon ends together at back. Sew top ribbon to top of bag. Cut an 8" length of ribbon for hanger; sew to each side of bag with a button. For flower, cut six 4" lengths of ribbon; tie a knot in center of each length. Form a loop with each ribbon length, stitching ends together at center to form flower. Work French Knots at center of flower; tack flower to gift bag.

Fig. 1

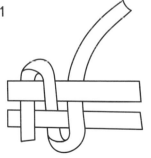

FLANNEL BAG

Enlarge the flannel bag pattern, page 146, by 200%. Follow instructions for *Flannel Bag Ornament*, above, changing ribbon lengths to three 11" ribbon lengths and a 39" length for woven band, and a 12" length of ribbon for handle.

spruce up a plain brown paper box with woven strips of homespun and ribbon ... hold them in place with double-stick tape. Add a festive ribbon bow and a gift tag made from a manila shipping tag, and you've got the **prettiest gift** under the tree!

Give us Lord, a bit o' sun,
a bit o' work
and a bit o' fun;
Give us all, in the struggle and sputter
Our daily bread and a bit o' butter.

— From an old inn in Lancaster, England

There's nothing quite as invigorating as a walk through the woods in the freshly fallen snow. Take along a basket and turn your walk into a treasure hunt. See what natural wonders you can gather to decorate your home... twigs of pine, cedar and holly, as well as colorful berries, pine cones and acorns are all fun finds. After you return home, take out a wooden bowl and line it with heavy-duty plastic wrap, then add water-soaked floral foam to create a base. Tuck the greenery and berry sprigs into the foam, making sure to let them overflow the bowl, then top with pine cones and acorns. For a burst of color, add apples or oranges. Be sure to water or mist as needed to keep your arrangement looking fresh.

So a-peeling...draw a design on an orange, lemon or lime using a felt tip marker. Carve along the marked design by removing the outside layer of the peel with a vegetable peeler or a lino tool from a hobby store. Stack several in a bowl or on a cake stand for a fragrant centerpiece.

HOLIDAY SWAG

Deck the halls, the windows, the china cabinet or anywhere else you want to spread holiday cheer! This striking swag will warm your home with the colors of Christmas. To make a more "scent-sational" version, use fresh greenery, berries and other jewels from Mother Nature. Decide how long you want your swag and cut two lengths of greenery that length. Wire the lengths together at the center and as necessary along the length. Wire berries along the center of the swag. Tear 1" wide strips of homespun...weave the strips and some ribbon through greenery. Tie a ribbon bow with streamers. Use wire to attach the bow to the center of the swag and it's ready to hang!

Make your holiday gatherings even more warm and cozy by dressing your table with a fabulous flannel runner. Finished off with woven ribbons and buttons, this table topper can be used all winter long. Coordinating chair back covers lend country charm.

CHAIR BACK COVERS

Match right sides and use a 1/2" seam allowance for all sewing unless otherwise indicated.

Measure from the seat of your chair, over the top of the chairback, and back down to the seat for the length of your chairback cover, then measure the width of your chair. Add 1" to these measurements then cut a piece of flannel and a piece of fabric for lining this size. Cut a piece of fabric 6" narrower than flannel piece; press long edges of fabric 1/2" to wrong side, then center on flannel piece and sew in place. Lay flannel piece on a flat surface; lay lengths of ribbon down the length and pin in place. Weave additional lengths of ribbon across flannel piece and pin in place. Sew ribbons in place using decorative stitches. Sew buttons along ribbons. Cut four lengths of ribbon for ties. With right sides together and leaving an opening for turning, sew flannel and lining together catching ends of ties in seams at edges of cover. Clip corners, turn right side out and press. Topstitch along edges of cover.

TABLE RUNNER

Match right sides and use a 1/2" seam allowance for all sewing unless otherwise indicated.

Cut two pieces of flannel the desired size for your runner. Lay one flannel piece on a flat surface; lay lengths of ribbon down the length of flannel piece and pin in place. Weave additional lengths of ribbon across flannel piece and pin in place. Sew ribbons in place using decorative stitches. Sew buttons along ribbons. With right sides together and leaving an opening at one end for turning, sew flannel pieces together. Clip corners, turn right side out and press. Topstitch along edges of runner.

Write *"Welcome One & All!"* on a big, black chalkboard and hang on the front door for a festive greeting…a strip of flannel makes the ideal hanger.

Snowflake Follies

*Combine a sleigh full of sparkles and glitter and you're guaranteed
to have a white Christmas! This tree is sure to delight anyone who longs each year
for that first snowfall. It's flocked with a flurry of trims. . .from cozy mitten ornaments
that will remind you of playful snowball fights to a garland of shimmering icicles.
And the forecast calls for even more fun when you make the other frosty projects,
including gift bags, cards, candleholders, a wall hanging and soaps!*

You'll have "snow" much fun crafting these wintry tree trims for the most creative holiday ever! Instructions for the Round Box Ornaments are on page 49.

ICICLE GARLAND

Transform your home into a Winter Wonderland with glistening icicle garland. Trace pattern, page 147, onto freezer paper, repeating as needed for desired length. Iron freezer paper onto cotton batting; cut out. Peel off paper pattern. Spray garland with spray adhesive; sprinkle with mica snow glitter; shake off excess and allow to dry. Spray lightly with matte acrylic sealer and allow to dry.

SOFT MITTEN ORNAMENTS

Continue the snowflake theme on your tree with mitten ornaments. . . you can also tuck a small gift inside each mitten for extra fun! Enlarge mitten pattern, page 148, 115%; cut out. Iron interfacing onto one side of cotton batting. For each mitten, use pattern to draw two mitten shapes

(one in reverse) onto interfaced side of batting. Cut out mittens; cut a 5"x7" piece from chenille for cuff. Trace small snowflake pattern, page 148, onto tracing paper and cut out; use pattern to cut a snowflake from blue felt. Using *French Knots and Straight Stitches*, pages 136-137, sew snowflake to front of one mitten shape. Sew a button to center of snowflake. With right sides matching and leaving wrist open, use a 1/2" seam allowance to sew mitten shapes together; clip curves. Sew short edges of cuff together. Matching wrong sides and long edges, fold cuff in half. Matching raw edges, slip cuff over mitten. Stitching through all layers, sew around top of mitten; turn mitten right side out then fold cuff to front. For hanger, tack ends of a length of ribbon inside mitten at sides.

SNOWFLAKE ORNAMENT

Polymer clay snowflakes sprinkled with mica snow glitter will add sparkle and shine to your tree. Read *Working with Polymer Clay*, page 137, then follow the polymer clay manufacturer's instructions to condition clay; run clay through a pasta machine (used for clay only) on the #1 setting. Using cookie cutters, cut out snowflakes. Following the instructions on the clay package, bake snowflakes in the oven. Once cooled, spray snowflakes with spray adhesive and sprinkle with mica snow glitter. Repeat on back of snowflake. Shake off excess glitter and allow to dry. Knot ends of a length of ribbon through snowflake and start decorating the tree!

CARDS WITH ENVELOPES AND TAGS

Think Snow! then gather up your snowflake stickers, ribbons, white and blue cardstock, and other papercrafting supplies to create your own wintery cards or tags for your gift bags. Mittens, sledding, icicles, a chance of flurries and thinking back to your childhood memories of the first snowfall of each year are sure to inspire your "cool" creations.

GIFT BAGS

Everyone will be saying Let it Snow! when you show up with this cascade of snow-studded gift bags. White textured bags topped with blue tissue paper and embellished with ribbons and snowflake stickers backed with blue felt, are a quick and easy way to turn your gift into a winter wonderland!

Trim packages with a homemade pompom in place of a bow. Wind yarn tightly around a 4-inch cardboard square several times. Slide yarn off cardboard and tie in the center with an 8-inch length of yarn. Clip the looped ends and shake out to fluff.

A pair of woolly mittens makes a sweet gift long after the goodies have been enjoyed. Stitch white buttons in a simple snowflake pattern on a pair of blue mittens and tuck packages of snack mix inside.

Line a new paint can with gingham fabric and wax paper, then fill with freshly baked cookies. . .what a clever way to share sweet treats!

Weather forecast for tonight:
DARK.
~ GEORGE CARLIN ~

ETCHED SNOWFLAKE CANDLE HOLDERS

Brighten your holidays with snowflakes and candlelight. Scatter snowflakes over plain glass candle holders simply by applying the negative area from a sheet of snowflake stickers to the glass; following the manufacturer's directions, brush etching cream onto the open area and then wash. Nestle each candle in a bank of snow created by pouring epsom salts into the base of each holder. Add embellishments of ribbons and charms around the neck of the candle holders, if desired.

Paper snowflakes cut from newspapers, brown paper bags or vintage maps turn a kid's room into a blizzard of holiday fun.

Let everyone know how you feel about snow! See page 130 to bring the frosty fun indoors with a trio of Snowflake Topiaries.

This cheerful wall hanging will remind you of fun-filled days spent playing in the snow.

SNOWFLAKE AND MITTEN WALL HANGING

1. Cut four 12" squares of white chenille and four 7" squares of blue felt. Tear four 8" squares of fabric. Trace snowflake and mitten patterns, page 148, onto tissue paper; cut out. Using patterns, cut two large snowflakes, four small snowflakes, and two mittens from white felt. Cut four 3½"x3" pieces of chenille for mitten cuffs.

2. Using French Knots and Long Stitches, page 136, sew a small snowflake to center of each mitten and each large snowflake; sew a button to center of each small snowflake.

3. Fold mitten cuffs in half lengthwise. Center mittens and cuffs on felt squares; glue in place with fabric glue.

4. Embellish large snowflakes with sequins and beads; center on remaining felt squares and glue in place.

5. With wrong sides matching, use a ½" seam allowance to sew chenille squares together leaving raw edges out.

6. Stamp wintery sayings on handmade paper; tear around words. Tear fabric strips slightly larger than stamped pieces.

7. Centering each decorated felt square on a torn fabric strip and layering a stamped piece on a torn rectangle of fabric, arrange pieces on chenille squares then hand stitch in place using decorative stitches. To complete wall hanging front, add embellishments such as buttons, sequins, beads, and ribbons . . . we used sequins with bead centers and extra large snaps for the centers of snowflakes we stitched on with floss.

8. Lay wall hanging front over a piece of batting and cut to size. Cut a piece of chenille to the same size. Layer pieces and stitch together at outside edges leaving raw edges.

9. For hanger, cut a length of batting 4" wide; fold in half lengthwise. Sew hanger to top of wall hanging.

10. Trace Icicle Garland pattern, page 147, onto freezer paper repeating as needed for length of wall hanging. Iron freezer paper onto cotton batting; cut out. Peel off paper pattern. Sew batting to bottom of wall hanging; spray with spray adhesive and sprinkle with mica snow glitter.

Snowflakes are each unique, one-of-a-kind creations. Now you can give a gift that's just as original…snowflake soaps! The flurries are fashioned from cookie cutters.

SNOWFLAKE SOAPS

Homemade soap shaped like snowflakes is a thoughtful and unique way to say "Happy Holidays!" To make snowflake soaps, look in your local craft store for loaf soap. Melt the soap according to the manufacturer's directions on the package; pour 1/4" into a plastic container sprayed with cooking oil. Before the soap totally hardens, turn the container over and carefully pop soap out onto wax paper. Use cookie cutters to cut snowflake shapes in soap. Allow soap to harden; clean edges as needed with a craft knife. Make a Round Box Ornament, page 49, without the hanger, to create a gift box. Nestle your snowflake soap in a bed of epsom salts and your gift is complete.

ROUND BOX ORNAMENTS

- green scrapbook paper
- blue scrapbook paper
- light-weight cardboard
- spray adhesive
- craft knife
- mica snow glitter
- small snowflake stickers
- chenille rick-rack
- sequins
- seed beads
- craft glue
- tracing paper

NOTE: *The following instructions make the Large Box Ornament. Use the measurements in parentheses for the Small Box Ornament. Use spray adhesive in a well-ventilated area.*

FOR BASE OF BOX:

1. For side of box, cut a 13$\frac{1}{2}$"x1$\frac{1}{4}$" (11"x$\frac{3}{4}$") strip from cardboard. For bottom of box, cut a 4" (3") dia. circle from cardboard.

2. Draw a line $\frac{1}{4}$" above bottom edge of cardboard strip; lightly score along line. Use craft knife to clip out wedges between raw edge and scored line.

Fig. 1

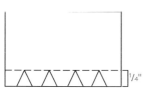

3. Wrapping a piece of scrapbook paper around raw edge of cardboard strip from scored line on front to scored line on back, cut a piece of scrapbook paper to cover cardboard strip. Cut a circle of scrapbook paper to cover box bottom. Use spray adhesive to adhere green scrapbook paper to pieces.

Fig. 2

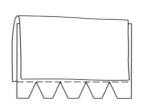

4. Fold strip along scored line and bend clipped edge to fit around box bottom. Glue clipped edge of strip around box bottom, overlapping clipped ends of strip.

5. Cut a 4" (3") dia. circle of scrapbook paper; glue to bottom of box to cover clipped edge.

FOR BOX TOP:

6. Repeat Steps 1-4, using blue scrapbook paper and the following measurements: 13$\frac{3}{4}$"x1" (11$\frac{1}{4}$"x$\frac{1}{2}$") strip for sides and 4$\frac{1}{4}$" (3$\frac{1}{4}$") dia. circle for bottom.

7. Cut a 4$\frac{1}{4}$" (3$\frac{1}{4}$") dia. circle of scrapbook paper; glue to box top to cover clipped edge.

8. Trace snowflake pattern, page 146, onto tracing paper; cut out. Use pattern to cut a snowflake from white felt. Adhere to top of box. Apply a snowflake sticker to center of felt snowflake.

9. Thin a small amount of craft glue with water; brush over top of box. Sprinkle mica snow glitter over glue; allow to dry, then tap off extra glitter.

10. Glue a length of rick-rack around sides of box top. For hanger, cut a 7" (6") length of rick-rack. Fold hanger in half; tack ends to rick-rack along sides of box. Tack a sequin and a seed bead to base of hanger.

Spray paint a paper-maché box blue; let dry. Add a Star of David to the lid using silver paint and when dry, fill the box with a dreidel and an equal amount of pennies or chocolate coins...kids love playing this game! Replace the lid and secure this pretty packaging with silver ribbon.

In about the same degree as you are helpful, you will be happy. ～ KARL REILAND

It's A Kids' Christmas!

Get your kids in on the fun of holiday decorating by teaching them origami. . .the Japanese art of paper folding. They'll love making their own tabletop Christmas tree, as well as pleated ornaments for the family evergreen. See pages 131-132 to make the Origami Tree and Ornaments.

KRINGLES CAN

Change an ordinary 3" can of Pringles® into an attractive, delectable gift that is sure to please young and old alike! Begin by melting Dipping Chocolate in the microwave according to manufacturer's instructions. Line a baking sheet with wax paper. Dip chips in chocolate and set on wax paper; refrigerate until chocolate coating hardens.

Cover can with yellow cardstock; glue a circle of red cardstock to lid. For label, cut a piece of vellum, then tear a larger piece of scrapbook paper for background. Write "Kringles" on the vellum; layer, then glue label to can. Use a 1/4" hole punch and a leaf punch to punch leaves and berries from scrapbook paper; glue to label. Place "chocolate chips" in can.

To make a snowman gift bag, fold down the top of a white lunch sack; round the edges of the folded-over flap with scissors. Add eyes and a mouth using a black pen and glue on an orange craft-foam nose. Top him off with an infant-size hat!

Kris Kringle will love to find these "chocolate chips" sitting out for him on Christmas Eve! The tasty treats also make great gifts for school friends and teachers. Dress up the original chip container to make your present even more festive.

I would be most content if my children grew up to be the kind of people who think decorating consists mostly of building enough *bookshelves.*

— Anna Quindlen •

Even little ones will love this clever craft. To create their own Wish List, they simply cut out pictures of the things they want and glue them on corrugated paper tags (instructions on page 132).

ACCORDION ALBUM

Cut two 4" squares from red mat board and a 24"x3⁷⁄₈" strip from green artist's paper. Accordion fold paper into six 4" squares. Working in a well-ventilated area, use spray adhesive to adhere a mat board square to the outside ends of the folded paper to create a cover for your album. Cut photo corners from craft foam; trim photographs to fit pages and secure in place using photo corners. Embellish album with craft foam shapes.

PLAYING CARD ALBUM

Collect a "full house" of memories using a deck of playing cards. All decked out with stickers and journaling, this album is the picture-perfect place to display your favorite family snapshots. Simply cover one side of several cards with assorted scrapbook papers then punch a hole in the upper corner of each card. On the covered side, add a photo and stickers along with some journaling. Tie the cards together with a ribbon tied into a bow. Embellish the front of your album as desired...we cut out pieces of left over playing cards and attached them using dimensional foam dots.

What fun! Colorful handprint tags add a personal touch to packages for everyone on your gift list. And they're so easy the whole family can make them! Draw around your hand onto colorful paper (like scrapbooking paper or craft paper) and cut out. Cut a rectangle from coordinating paper to make a cuff for a boy's hand. Glue on tinsel pom-poms for rings or a bracelet on a girl's hand. If you'd like, make a hole for the hanger near the cuff or bracelet and thread embroidery floss through it, tying the ends into a knot to hang from the present. Don't forget to write the "to" and "from" information on the tag before attaching it to your gift!

Take note of this fun project! The Notepad Booklet is great for jotting down phone numbers, important reminders, and more. You'll find the instructions on page 133.

CHRISTMAS
is for
Sharing

Handmade gifts can't help but get noticed! Because they show how much you care, they're sure to be appreciated. A warm & cozy fleece scarf is ready in a jiffy for someone special. Family & friends will love a whimsical mug cozy, fun wire bookmarks, or a sentimental paperweight. And don't forget your four-legged friends. Our dog quilt and cat bed will soon be your pets' favorite places to snuggle.

Something for everyone on your Christmas list! These gifts from the heart are oh-so thoughtful and will be treasured for years to come. Instructions begin on page 56.

Made with ♥YOU♥ in Mind

The jolly old elf, himself, would like to see this Santa Doll under the tree. Any little girl will love a sweet, rosy sweater or one with a playful snowman. Instructions for these festive gifts are found on pages 133-134.

"So remember while December brings the only Christmas Day, in the year let there be Christmas in the things you do and say."
— Anonymous

"Christmas is doing a little something extra for someone."
— Charles Schultz

There is Glory in a great mistake.
—Nathalia Crane.

EMBELLISHED GLOVES

The design on these knitted gloves is done with a technique called duplicate stitch using embroidery floss. Duplicate stitch is a V-shaped stitch worked over the weave of the knitting (Fig. 1). For placement of stitches, follow the chart on page 154. Leave a 3" tail at the beginning and ending of your stitching. To secure the stitches, thread the needle with one of the tails, run it under several stitches, then go back under several stitches in the opposite direction; trim tail.

Repeat to secure the rest of the tails. To complete each stitch, come up at 1, go down at 2, come up at 3, and go back down at 1.

Fig. 1

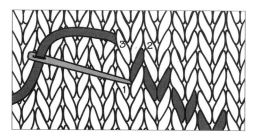

FLEECE SCARF

Whip up this gift as quick as quick can be. Cut a 7"x63" piece of fleece for the body of your scarf. Layer pieces of assorted colors of fleece 3" from each end to create your design. Using invisible thread, machine sew zigzag stitches to secure edges of pieces in place. We used a diamond pattern, but you could pick something as simple as stripes. Cut ½" wide strips in ends for fringe.

hot CoCoA MOCHA

...a yummy cocoa mix to give along with your mug cozy!

3 c. hot cocoa mix
½ c. instant coffee
¾ t. cinnamon
½ c. mini marshmallows

Mix hot cocoa mix, instant coffee and spice together. Store in an airtight container. Give mix & marshmallows with serving instructions:

Add 3 tablespoons mix to ⅔ cup boiling water.

MUG COZY

Refer to Embroidery Stitches, pages 136-137, before beginning.

Wash an old sweater in hot water, then dry it on hot to create felted wool. Cut a piece of felted wool to fit around your mug. Using the pattern on page 154, follow *Making Patterns*, page 134, to trace the snowman pattern onto tracing paper. Use the pattern to cut snowman from white felt. Use two strands of grey embroidery floss to work *French Knots* for eyes and six strands of orange floss to work a *Straight Stitch* for nose. Using two strands of white floss, work *Blanket Stitches* along edges of snowman to secure it near one end of wool piece. Use two strands of grey floss to work *Back Stitches* for arms. For snow, use two strands of white floss to work scattered *Cross Stitches* around snowman. Using six strands of green floss, work a running stitch along top and bottom edges of cozy. Sew three buttons along one side edge of cozy; tacked on the other side edge, form loops with embroidery floss for closures. Wrap cozy around mug, loop closures around buttons. Pour yourself a cup of hot cocoa, sit back and relax!

Need a quick hostess gift? Use a dainty, flea-market find teacup and tuck in a little herb plant. Wrap it up in cellophane and add a jolly note...easy, sweet and long lasting!

TRAVEL JEWELRY BOX

- 4$\frac{1}{2}$"x4$\frac{1}{2}$"x2$\frac{1}{2}$" papier-mâché box with lid
- travel rubber stamps
- brown ink
- light brown ink
- scrapbook paper with lettering
- travel stickers
- metal letters
- black felt
- light-weight cardboard
- shank buttons
- craft glue

Tear an approximately 4" square of scrapbook paper; glue to box lid. Use light brown ink to darken edges of box, lid, and paper square. Use both inks to stamp various travel sayings on box and lid. Adhere stickers and metal letters to lid of box. For inside of box, cut a 4" square of felt; glue to inside bottom of box. Cut a 2$\frac{1}{2}$"x16" strip of felt; glue around insides of box. For dividers, cut 3$\frac{7}{8}$" squares from cardboard and felt; glue squares of felt to both sides of each square. Sew a shank button to the center of each covered square. Insert dividers into box.

TRAVEL TRAY

This travel tray is an useful and unique way for travelers to keep their keys, pocket change, and jewelry together while away from home. The sides of the tray untie to lay flat in your suitcase. To create yours, cut one 8$\frac{1}{2}$"x11" piece each of cotton fabric and flannel, three 8$\frac{1}{2}$"x11" pieces of low-loft batting, and four 8" lengths of $\frac{3}{8}$"w satin ribbon. Matching right sides and raw edges, place fabric pieces together; stack batting on top of the fabric pieces. Using a $\frac{1}{2}$" seam allowance, leaving an opening for turning, and catching a ribbon end in the seam (approximately 1$\frac{1}{4}$" from each corner) sew pieces together. Turn right side out and sew opening closed. Topstitch, through all layers, 1$\frac{1}{4}$" from edges and your travel tray is ready to pack. When you reach your destination, tie the ribbons together at each corner to create the sides on your travel tray and you're ready to empty your pockets!

"It isn't the holly; it isn't the snow. It isn't the tree, nor the firelight's glow. It's the warmth that comes to the hearts of men when the Christmas spirit returns again."
— Anonymous

BOOKMARKS

Colorful beads make these bookmarks extra special. For each marker, thread four small beads onto a length of 18-gauge craft wire. Bend the wire on each side of the beads to hold beads in place. Form bends in the remainder of the wire, then curl the ends to finish. For dangles, add a small bead, a large bead, then a small bead to a eyepin; bend end in a loop around marker between small beads; if necessary, use wire cutters to trim wire.

"Books are the quietest and most constant of friends; they are the most accessible and wisest of counselors, and the most patient of teachers."
— Charles W. Eliot

PAPERWEIGHT

This paperweight is a gift that Dad can proudly display on his desk. Invert a clear glass ashtray onto craft foam; draw around the ashtray onto the foam and cut out. Repeat with a photograph. Use craft glue to glue photo to craft foam. Add names to photo, if desired, using alphabet tiles or stickers. If using alphabet tiles, make sure tiles will be in the bowl area of the ashtray and not along the edges. Invert ashtray on photo and use craft glue to adhere in place. Embellish paperweight with clear adhesive phrases, tags, and a ribbon.

Tie lengths of tulle around packages and position bows along the narrow or front side of the gift instead of top and center...great for stacking presents.

Everywhere, we learn only from those whom we love.
- JOHANN WOLFGANG VON GOETHE -

Animals are such agreeable friends

— they ask no questions, they pass no criticisms.

— GEORGE ELIOT

DOGGY QUILT

- red corduroy for quilt blocks
- heavy-duty washable fabric for quilt blocks
- heavy-duty washable fabric for backing
- high-loft polyester batting
- embroidery floss

Use a 1/2" seam allowance for all sewing unless otherwise indicated.

For blocks, cut ten 9" squares each from red corduroy and heavy-duty fabric. Alternating fabrics, sew four squares together to make a row. Sew five rows together to make quilt top. Matching right sides and raw edges, place quilt top and backing together; stack batting on top of the fabric pieces. Leaving an opening for turning, sew pieces together. Clip edges and turn right side out; sew opening closed. Sew floss ties at intersections of each block, through all layers. Tie floss in a knot; leave strings long.

Take your animals to the pet store for some fun holiday shopping. Take along a notepad so you can make your pets a "wish list."

CAT BED

- ½ yard beige fleece
- ½ yard plaid fabric
- cream and red felt
- beige, green, red, and black embroidery floss
- 8" dia. circle of 3" thick foam rubber
- 6"x40" piece of 2" thick foam rubber
- spray adhesive

Use a ½" seam allowance for all sewing unless otherwise indicated. Refer to Embroidery Stitches, pages 136-137, before beginning.

1. For sides of cat bed, cut a 13"x41" strip of fleece; sew ends together. Using spray adhesive in a well-ventilated area, adhere ends of 6"x40" piece of foam together. Wrap fleece around 6"x40" piece of foam; sew edges of fleece together with the seam along the inside bottom edge of cat bed.

2. For bottom of cat bed, cut two 14" dia. circles from plaid fabric. Matching right sides and raw edges, place circles together. Leaving an opening for turning, sew circles together. Clip edges and turn the cover right side out. Insert the circle of foam into the cover; sew opening closed. Insert bed bottom into center of cat bed.

3. Using the patterns on page 154, follow *Making Patterns*, page 134, to trace the patterns onto tracing paper, cut out. Use the patterns to cut cat from cream felt and letters to spell "KITTY" from red felt. Work *Satin Stitches*, with red floss for cat's nose; work black *French Knots* for cat's eyes. Attach cat to side of bed by working green *Straight Stitches* for cat's whiskers. Work beige *Running Stitches* along edges of letters to attach to bed.

Here Kitty★Kitty cookies

1 PKG. ACTIVE DRY YEAST
¼ C. WARM WATER
1 C. ALL-PURPOSE FLOUR
1 ENV. UNFLAVORED GELATIN MIX
1 C. POWDERED MILK
¼ C. CORN OIL
1 EGG
6-0Z. CAN TUNA
¼ C. WATER

DISSOLVE YEAST IN WARM WATER; SET ASIDE. COMBINE FLOUR, GELATIN MIX & MILK IN MIXING BOWL; STIR IN YEAST, OIL, EGG, TUNA & WATER. STIR 'TIL WELL BLENDED. DROP DOUGH BY HALF-TEASPOONFULS ONTO UNGREASED BAKING SHEETS. BAKE AT 300 DEGREES FOR 25 MINUTES. COOL COMPLETELY ∽ STORE IN REFRIGERATOR. MAKES 8 TO 10 DOZEN.

Don't limit your creativity to the gift. Take it a step further and make a clever container, too! From whimsical to elegant, this charming assortment of gift wraps is simple and fun to make. Turn corrugated cardboard into a Pillow Gift Box and tie with a pretty bow. . .so easy! The Cone Gift Box and Gift Card Holder can be made to please anyone by choosing the perfect scrapbook paper design. And a Santa Pocket Envelope is just right for homemade "coupon" books.

CONE GIFT BOX

The Country Friends embellished their Cone Gift Box with buttons to match their scrapbook paper, but you could use other embellishments such as charms or stickers or leave it plain. Enlarge or reduce the pattern, page 155, to create gift boxes of different sizes. With all the types of scrapbook papers that are available, the possibilities are endless! Kate wants to let you know this cone isn't suited for ice cream!

Use spray adhesive (in a well-ventilated area) to adhere a sheet of scrapbook paper to a piece of Bristol board. Photocopy pattern, page 155; cut out. Tape pattern to back of covered board. Cut out pattern along solid lines and fold along dotted lines; remove pattern then glue sides together. Use a hole punch to punch a hole in each side of box. For handle, thread the ends of a length of wire-edged ribbon through holes then knot on inside to secure. Randomly, glue buttons to cone. For closure, glue one end of a length of ribbon to under side of lid; wrap remaining end around a button to secure.

Collect old jars & covered bowls to fill with candy gifts.

There are some days when I think I'm going to die from an overdose of satisfaction. — SALVADOR DALI —

Dress up gift cards by crafting handmade holders from scrapbook paper. See page 132 for instructions for the Santa Pocket Envelope shown below.

PILLOW GIFT BOX

Enlarge or reduce pattern, page 157, for desired size box; cut out. Tape pattern to back of a piece of corrugated craft paper; cut out shape and slit in shape then score lightly along dashed lines. Remove pattern and fold gift box into pillow shape; insert flap into slit then tie closed with a length of ribbon. Cut a tag from craft paper and punch a small hole near top of tag then thread a length of string through hole to tie tag to ribbon. Apply "JOY" stickers to buttons then use dimensional foam dots to adhere buttons to tag.

GIFT CARD HOLDER

Use spray adhesive in a well-ventilated area.

Cut a 7³/₄"x2⁷/₈" rectangle from white cardstock and scrapbook paper; use spray adhesive to adhere papers together. Score holder 3³/₄" from one end; fold along score mark. For closure, use craft knife to cut a small "V" in paper (Fig. 1). Scuff up edges of scrapbook paper with sandpaper. Cut a square of white cardstock slightly larger than beaded snowflake sticker then trim with decorative-edge craft scissors. Cut a square of green cardstock larger than the white one. Layer and glue squares together; center and glue to front of holder. Use a dimensional foam dot to adhere sticker to center of white square. Cut a narrow strip of green cardstock; glue to end of holder. Use double-stick tape to secure gift card inside holder.

Fig. 1

4"

3³/₄"

EMBOSSING GIFT WRAP, CARDS AND SIMPLE-TO-MAKE PROJECTS

The Country Friends love to emboss! Holly loves the way embossing dresses up the cards she makes, Mary Elizabeth likes to emboss gift bags and tags for her baked goods, and Kate likes playing with the embossing heat tool.

Holly and Mary Elizabeth promise that embossing is as easy as these four simple steps. The most important thing to remember is that you have to apply the embossing powder while the ink is still wet.

1. Stamp your image. Mary Elizabeth likes to add accents with an embossing marker, like the green border on the poinsettia card. (Work with one color at a time.)

2. Sprinkle embossing powder over the image while the ink is still wet.

3. Lightly tap excess powder off image.

4. Heat image with an embossing heat tool until powder melts and turns shiny. It's magic!

Create nostalgic ornaments that are miniature works of art. Pull out that box filled with Christmas cards you've received over the years, then give the cards a place of honor on your evergreen. Trim each scene as desired, then back the card cutout with a paper doily. Embellish with charms, ribbon roses, scraps of ribbon tied into bows or other pretty trims.

Does Santa Claus have time to send Christmas Cards?

PHOTO WRAPPING PAPER

Bring back memories and make personalized wrapping paper at the same time! Simply photocopy several photos, side-by-side, all at once, then print on the largest paper possible. Use the paper to wrap your gifts, piecing paper as necessary to cover larger packages.

Recycle your shoe boxes into handy holiday storage containers. Spray paint the boxes with your favorite holiday colors. Cover the lid with Christmas cards and finish by adding a decorative trim around the edge.

"The best of all gifts around any Christmas tree: the presence of a happy family all wrapped up in each other."

— Burton Hillis

Perhaps the best yuletide decoration
is being wreathed in smiles.
— UNKNOWN —

CRAFT FOAM CONTAINERS

Enlarge or reduce pattern, page 154, to make desired size container; cut out. Tape pattern to a piece of craft foam. Cut out shape. Use a small hole punch to punch a hole at end of each point. Place gift at center of craft foam. Bend points toward center; lace ribbon through holes and tie in a bow. To embellish your container, punch or cut circles or other designs from fun foam; glue to container. . .you can also buy pre-cut, self-adhesive shapes to decorate with.

Transform a window box into a Christmas garden with young potted evergreens, such as short-needle pines and blue spruce, which can be planted in the yard later. Be sure to select trees that are tall enough to be enjoyed from indoors as well as out, then fill in with real or faux plants and berries.

Cheery holiday potholders with pockets can be found at any kitchen store. When filled with Crispy-Crunchy Crouton Sticks (recipe is on page 74) and a few favorite dip recipes, they're handy keep-on-hand gifts.

"We make a living by what we get, we make a life by what we give."
— Sir Winston Churchill

Tasteful offerings

*T*his year, give gifts that your family and friends will rave over! Holly, Mary Elizabeth and Kate have been busy in the kitchen cooking up some tasty treats. From savory pita snacks for munching to scrumptious granola for crunching, these recipes will have friends asking for more. And for an extra measure of homemade cheer, deliver your presents in containers you've either crafted or decorated yourself.

Joyful holidays begin with gifts for every taste. Trimming-the-Tree Pita Snacks, Cranberry-Chip Cookies, Homemade Maple Syrup and other taste-tempting treats make up this delectable collection. In addition to great recipes, you'll also find fun and easy ways to present your goodies.

friends
TO:
Bradfords
FROM:
Hensons

Merry Christmas

homemade
maple
syrup

BARLEY QUICK BREAD

In November of 2000, my sisters and I traveled to Finland to see the town where our ancestors had once lived. Prior to leaving, we collected letters from some of the children in our hometown to take to Santa Claus. It was there in Santa's kitchen at Santa Park that we enjoyed this delicious bread. We will always cherish the memory of Santa's kindness and the sweet aroma of freshly baked Finnish bread.

2 c. all-purpose flour
$^{1}/_{2}$ c. pearled barley, uncooked
1 t. salt
1 t. sugar
1 t. baking powder
$^{1}/_{2}$ t. baking soda
1 c. buttermilk
$^{1}/_{4}$ c. butter, melted

Mix together first 6 ingredients; stir in buttermilk. Turn dough onto a lightly-floured surface; knead. Roll dough into an oval shape, $^{1}/_{2}$ to $^{3}/_{4}$-inch thick. Score dough with a knife and prick with a fork; place on a lightly greased and floured baking sheet. Bake at 375 degrees for 15 to 25 minutes. Cool on a wire rack and brush with melted butter. Serves 4 to 6.

Sherry Saarinen
Hancock, MI

OH GOODIE! IT'S

APPLE SYRUP

Re-warm in the microwave & serve over pancakes!

1 c. UNSWEETENED APPLE JUICE
1 c. SUGAR
$^{1}/_{4}$ c. APPLE LIQUEUR
1 CINNAMON STICK

...great over vanilla ice cream!

Combine all ingredients in a saucepan over medium heat. Bring to a boil, stirring constantly, and boil for about 15 minutes or until slightly thickened. Remove from heat and pour, including the cinnamon stick, into a sterilized 12-ounce bottle. Cap tightly and refrigerate up to one week.   Cindy Lawrence ★ Topeka, KS

December will always be a most special month for me. In past years, we anticipated the arrival of family & friends by spending many hours baking cookies and candies and decorating our home both inside and out. But December 2000 will always be the most precious of all. After spending 22 days in a foreign country, my husband and I returned home just in time for Christmas with not one, but two babies! What a wonderful gift we were given! We were able to share with our family their two new grandsons, nephews and cousins. This arrival was truly a miracle and brought back the real reason we celebrate Christmas to the front of our family celebrations.

— Beth Hoffman
Santa Claus, IN

"Good bread is the most fundamentally satisfying of all foods; and good bread with fresh butter, the greatest of feasts."

— James Beard

"The smell of good bread baking, like the sound of lightly flowing water, is indescribable in its evocation of innocence and delight."

— M.F.K. Fisher,
The Art of Eating

"In cooking, as in all the arts, simplicity is the sign of perfection."
— Curnonsky

Even when freshly washed and relieved of all obvious confections, cHildren tend to be STicky.

—FRAN LEBOWITZ—

HOMEMADE MAPLE SYRUP

I always keep a batch in my fridge…it's yummy!

4 c. sugar
2 T. corn syrup
1/2 c. brown sugar, packed
2 c. water
1 t. vanilla extract
1 t. maple flavoring

Stir together first 4 ingredients in a saucepan until sugar dissolves. Heat over medium heat until boiling; boil one to 2 minutes. Remove from heat and cool 5 to 10 minutes. Stir in vanilla and maple flavoring. Makes about 4 cups.

*Jana Warnell
Kalispell, MT*

Tuck pancake mix into a basket along with a bottle of Homemade Maple Syrup, a new extra-large spatula and some flavored teabags. Any busy family will enjoy this breakfast treat.

SYRUP BOTTLE

For each label (one for each side of container), use a 2¼" circle punch to punch a circle from corrugated olive craft paper and a 1½" circle punch to punch a circle from natural paper. To create your label, stamp "maple syrup" on natural circle and handwrite "homemade" above stamp; layer and glue circles together. Use a ½" hole punch to punch "berries" from red cardstock and a holly leaf punch to punch a leaf from green cardstock. Glue leaf and berries at top of label. To attach labels, punch a ⅛" hole on each side of both labels. Weave a length of ribbon through the holes; remove spout from syrup bottle and slip label over bottle then knot ribbon and trim ends behind a label. Add syrup and replace spout.

Get that special someone's day off to a great start with a real breakfast treat…Homemade Maple Syrup. The oh-so-sweet topping will make Christmas morning pancakes or waffles even more tasty.

BROWN SUGAR GRANOLA

Decorate a brown paper bag and fill with this yummy snack...so handy to nibble on while traveling to visit family.

2 T. butter
1/4 c. corn syrup
1/4 c. honey
2 3/4 c. quick-cooking oats,
   uncooked
1/2 c. sliced almonds
1/2 c. brown sugar, packed
1 1/2 t. cinnamon
1/2 c. flaked coconut, toasted

Melt butter with corn syrup and honey in a small saucepan; set aside. Combine remaining ingredients except coconut in a large bowl; blend in butter mixture. Spread in a well-greased 13"X9" baking pan; press firmly to pack. Bake at 350 degrees until dark and golden, about 20 to 30 minutes; turn onto aluminum foil to cool. Break into bite-size pieces; mix in coconut. Store in an airtight container. Makes 1 1/4 pounds.

*O*nce upon a time, on a snowy day when I was very young, Mom was in the kitchen making her heavenly potato soup. Taking her eyes off the soup for just a minute, she asked my brother Bob and me if we knew where snowflakes came from...and then she told us angels in heaven are having a pillow fight. Now every time it snows I think of angels, Mom and her potato soup.
        — Dianne Selep
         Warren, OH

Make Brown Sugar Granola, and you'll have holiday snacking all wrapped up. Transform a plain brown bag into a jolly gift sack with scrapbook paper and a few other trims. Pack the crunchy munchies inside and it's ready to go.

EMBELLISHED BROWN BAG

Use spray adhesive for all gluing unless otherwise indicated. Use spray adhesive in a well-ventilated area.

Using decorative-edge craft scissors, cut a piece of black scrapbook paper 1/4" smaller on all sides than front of a lunch-size brown bag. Cut a piece of red scrapbook paper 1/2" smaller on all sides than front of bag. Using spray adhesive, adhere papers together, then to front of bag.

Fold top of bag down to form a 3" flap. Cut a 1 1/2" wide strip of black scrapbook paper and tear a 1" wide strip of newsprint scrapbook paper to fit across flap; glue papers together, then to flap. Use craft glue to glue a length of chenille rick-rack to underside of flap so it peeks out from underneath; glue a length of ribbon across newsprint. Embellish with buttons, bells and thin jute. Make handmade black rimmed tags from cardstock. Write greeting then punch holes for jute tie and glue to bag.

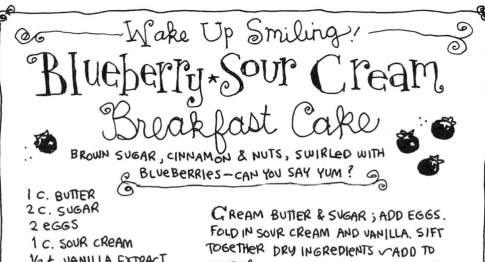

Wake Up Smiling!
Blueberry ★ Sour Cream Breakfast Cake

BROWN SUGAR, CINNAMON & NUTS, SWIRLED WITH BLUEBERRIES—CAN YOU SAY YUM?

1 c. BUTTER
2 c. SUGAR
2 EGGS
1 c. SOUR CREAM
½ t. VANILLA EXTRACT
2 c. CAKE FLOUR
¼ t. SALT
1 t. BAKING POWDER
½ c. BLUEBERRIES, WELL DRAINED

GARNISH: POWDERED SUGAR

CREAM BUTTER & SUGAR; ADD EGGS. FOLD IN SOUR CREAM AND VANILLA. SIFT TOGETHER DRY INGREDIENTS; ADD TO MIXTURE. FOLD IN BLUEBERRIES. POUR ⅓ BATTER INTO A GREASED & FLOURED BUNDT® PAN; SPRINKLE WITH HALF THE FILLING. POUR ⅓ BATTER OVER TOP; SPRINKLE WITH REMAINING FILLING. TOP WITH REMAINING BATTER. GENTLY SWIRL CAKE WITH A SPATULA. BAKE AT 350 DEGREES FOR ONE HOUR. COOL AND INVERT ONTO A SERVING PLATTER. DUST WITH POWDERED SUGAR. SERVES 12 TO 16.

FILLING:
½ c. BROWN SUGAR, PACKED
1 t. CINNAMON
½ c. CHOPPED NUTS
MIX UNTIL COMBINED.

A RECIPE FROM LAVERNE FANG ★ JOLIET, IL

PECAN MINI MUFFINS

Just the right size for little fingers to pick up and enjoy!

1 c. brown sugar, packed
⅓ c. all-purpose flour
⅛ t. salt
1 c. chopped pecans
2 eggs
½ t. vanilla extract

Mix all ingredients by hand just until moist. Divide dough into mini muffin tins coated with non-stick vegetable spray. Bake at 350 degrees for 20 minutes. Immediately remove muffins from pans and cool on wire racks. Makes 2 dozen.

Tisha Brown
Elizabethtown, PA

Granny used to make homemade biscuits for our family breakfast each Christmas morning. One year, we decided to save her the work and bought biscuits at a fast food restaurant the day before; however, not everyone in the family was in on this little secret. As we ate breakfast my cousin said, "Granny, these are the best biscuits you've ever made!" My how we all laughed! For the record, although she didn't use a recipe, Granny did make the best biscuits in the world.

— Robin Wilson
Altamonte Springs, FL

TRIMMING-THE-TREE PITA SNACKS

Add variety...sprinkle with bacon bits, diced pepperoni, dried tomatoes or any other favorite "trimmings."

8 pita rounds
olive oil
2/3 c. grated Parmesan cheese
4 t. dried basil
1 t. garlic powder

Carefully split pitas into 2 rounds; slice each round into 6 wedges. Arrange wedges smooth-side up on aluminum foil-lined baking sheets; brush lightly with olive oil. Flip wedges over; brush with olive oil. Set aside. Combine cheese, basil and garlic powder; sprinkle evenly over wedges. Bake at 350 degrees for 12 to 14 minutes; remove to a wire rack to cool completely. Makes 16 servings.

Like a lot of mothers, I don't measure ingredients when I bake or cook...it's always been a pinch of this, a scoop of that. One day, my daughter asked me how she was ever going to learn to cook when I didn't write anything down. From that day on, I began to measure ingredients and wrote each recipe down. It took me most of the year but, by Christmas, I had completed her cookbook. I can still see the look of joy on her face as she leafed through it. What a wonderful way to preserve family recipes.

—Sally Davis
Payne, OH

Give a gift of Trimming-the-Tree Pita Snacks and you're likely to start a new holiday tradition. Decorating for Christmas can work up quite an appetite...these crunchy treats are just the answer!

Make a Trimming The Tree Snack Box

Unfold a cake box and apply spray adhesive to the right side... now smooth the box onto the wrong side of a piece of wrapping paper.

Use a craft knife to trim the paper along the sides of the box and cut through the slits. Cut a 3" square "window" in lid of box. Cover window from wrong side with clear cellophane.

Ok! Now refold the box. Add a length of ribbon, then a length of fringe trim to the flap. Embellish box lid with scrapbook paper pieces, photo corners, stickers, buttons, brads and a homemade tag. Place your pita snacks inside!

ZESTY MOZZARELLA CHEESE BITES

A tasty take-along nibbler.

16-oz. pkg. mozzarella cheese
1/4 c. roasted garlic oil
2 t. balsamic vinegar
2 T. fresh basil, chopped
1 T. whole mixed peppercorns,
    coarsely ground

Cube cheese into 1/2-inch cubes; place in a medium mixing bowl. Set aside. Whisk remaining ingredients together; pour over cheese cubes. Toss to coat; cover and refrigerate up to 3 days. Makes 14 servings.

PAINTED GIFT TIN

Paint a cream stripe along the top of a small tin pail; allow to dry, then paint a smaller green stripe in center of cream stripe. Thread a length of red jute through two buttons; sliding buttons to sides of pail, glue a button to each side of pail and tie jute in a bow in the front. Cut a tag from orange cardstock; embellish with a "friends" charm and a small piece of ribbon, then personalize tag. Thread jute through a hole in tag, then attach to pail with dimensional foam dots.

Give your favorite cheese lover a sumptuous surprise this Christmas. Lightly coated with fresh basil and ground peppercorns, the Zesty Mozzarella Cheese Bites have just the right zip.

A laugh is a smile that bursts.
—MARY WALDRIP—

Do something that makes you giggle:

* take silly pictures wearing Santa hats!

* sit on red and green balloons!

* paint your toe nails red and green!

* watch a funny holiday movie with the kids!

Croutons aren't just for salads. The perfect size for dipping, these Crispy-Crunchy Crouton Sticks are a great alternative to chips and crackers. Put them in decorated cellophane bags and keep them on hand for drop-in guests.

CRISPY-CRUNCHY CROUTON STICKS

These big dunkers are just right for dips, spreads and even soups.

8-oz. loaf French baguette
1/2 c. butter
1 T. fresh basil, chopped
1/4 t. garlic powder
1/8 t. onion salt

Slice baguette in half horizontally; cut widthwise into one-inch wide sticks. Set aside. Melt butter in a 12" skillet; stir in basil, garlic powder and onion salt. Add half the crouton sticks; sauté until coated. Arrange in a single layer in an ungreased jelly-roll pan; repeat with remaining crouton sticks. Bake at 300 degrees for 25 to 30 minutes; flip crouton sticks halfway through baking. Cool completely. Store in an airtight container up to 3 days or freeze up to 3 months. Makes 2 dozen.

*C*hristmas in our family is the best time to bake all those wonderful recipes that have been passed down from generation to generation or even from friend to friend. Sometimes the aromas bring back the most wonderful memories and hopefully create more for those new little ones around us.

— Rosalie Colby
Hiram, ME

Polka Dot Bag

Punch assorted sizes of circles from red scrapbook paper. Use alphabet stamps to stamp the name of food item on some of the circles. Use double-sided tape or glue dots to adhere the circles to a cellophane bag. Add crouton sticks to the bag; tucking in a sprig of berries and adding a gift tag, tie bag closed with a length of pretty ribbon!

MUSTARD JAR

Cut a circle of scrapbook paper to fit top of lid. Use craft glue to glue circle to lid; glue a length of natural jute along edges of circle. For label, cut a strip of plain cardstock long enough to wrap around jar and overlap, then cut a wider strip of scrapbook paper. Use a paint pen to write "MUSTARD" on cardstock strip, then use a fine-point pen to write "sweet" on one side and "tangy" on the other side. Center and glue cardstock strip to paper strip; glue label to jar. Glue lengths of jute along top and bottom edges of label. Add short pieces of ribbon and buttons to resemble a cluster of holly berries and leaves.

*B*undle up a bag of home-baked cookies in a holiday apron and tie with a length of rick-rack. Fill the apron pocket with the recipe and a cookie cutter or two. The happy baker will be oh-so pleased.

Sweet and Tangy Mustard is a treat for the taste buds! The unique blend of mustard, sweetened condensed milk, horseradish and Worcestershire sauce makes a zesty dip and will also add zip to sandwiches.

Sweet and Tangy Mustard

Give a bag of pretzels with this tasty dip!

14-oz. can sweetened condensed milk

8-oz. jar mustard

2 T. prepared horseradish

2 T. Worcestershire sauce

★

Stir all ingredients together; spoon into an airtight container. Refrigerate up to 3 months. Makes 3 cups.

~Hope Davenport
Portland, TX

MILK

Condensed milk is wonderful. I don't see HOW they can get a cow to sit down on those little cans.
-FRED ALLEN-

CRANBERRY-CHIP COOKIE MIX

A new spin...substitute dried strawberries!

1$\frac{1}{8}$ c. all-purpose flour
$\frac{1}{2}$ c. quick-cooking oats,
    uncooked
$\frac{1}{2}$ t. baking soda
$\frac{1}{2}$ t. salt
$\frac{1}{3}$ c. brown sugar, packed
$\frac{1}{3}$ c. sugar
$\frac{1}{2}$ c. dried cranberries
$\frac{1}{2}$ c. white chocolate chips
$\frac{1}{2}$ c. chopped walnuts

Mix all ingredients; pour into a one-quart plastic zipping bag; close bag. Place bag and baking instructions in gift bag.

Instructions: Cream together $\frac{1}{2}$ cup softened butter, one egg and one teaspoon vanilla extract in a medium bowl. Add bag contents; mix until well blended. Drop by rounded teaspoonfuls onto greased baking sheets. Bake at 350 degrees for 8 to 10 minutes or until the edges turn golden. Cool on wire racks. Makes about 3 dozen.

Lynne Takayesu-Wulfestieg
Downely, CA

Share the joy of holiday baking with our Cranberry-Chip Cookie Mix. Packed with cranberries, white chocolate chips and walnuts, these cookies are berry delicious! Tuck a batch of mix into a wintry fabric bag, and don't forget to include the directions.

FABRIC BAG

Match right sides and use a $\frac{1}{2}$" seam allowance for all sewing.

Cut a 7"x27" piece of white canvas. Press short edges $\frac{1}{2}$" to wrong side; sew in place. Matching right sides and raw edges and referring to Fig. 1, fold fabric to middle. Pin edges of body together; finger press fold of flap, then turn flap to right side. For snowflakes on flap, leaving 1" along sides unadorned and sewing through top of flap only, use two strands of white embroidery floss to work Straight Stitches to make four snowflakes; work French Knots to attach sequins to flap and to centers of Straight Stitches. Turn flap back, as in Fig. 1; pin edges of flap in place. Sew along long edges of bag. For flat bottom bag, match bottom side seams to bottom; sew across each corner 1" from point, Fig. 2. Turn right side out. Use fabric glue to glue a doubled length of white pom-pom fringe across underside of flap. Adorn a white tag with sequin snowflakes; attach to bag with a length of floss.

Fig. 1

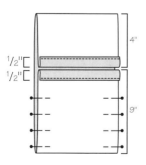

Fig. 2

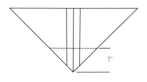

HOLLY JOLLY COOKIES

Almost too pretty to eat!

1³/₄ c. all-purpose flour
1¹/₂ t. baking powder
¹/₂ t. salt
¹/₂ c. shortening
1 c. sugar
1 egg
³/₄ t. vanilla extract
¹/₄ t. almond extract
¹/₄ c. finely chopped
    blanched almonds
1 egg white, beaten
green decorating sugar
red cinnamon candies

Stir together flour, baking powder
and salt; set aside. In a separate
bowl, cream shortening; gradually
add sugar, beating until fluffy.
Blend in egg, vanilla and almond
extract. Fold in almonds. Stir in
dry ingredients; chill mixture for
3 hours. Divide dough in half and
roll out each half between 2 sheets
of wax paper to ¹/₈-inch thickness.
Cut out cookies with a leaf-shape
cutter. Arrange leaves in groups
of 2 or 3 on an ungreased baking
sheet; brush surfaces with egg
white. Sprinkle green sugar over
top of cookies and place
3 to 4 cinnamon candies at the
base of the leaves. Bake at
375 degrees for 8 to 10 minutes.
Cool on wire racks. Makes 3 dozen.

Kathy McLaren
Visalia, CA

*"Christmas! The very word brings
joy to our hearts."*
— Joan Winmill Brown

Holly Plates

Holly loves to personalize gift plates for
giving goodies to friends. She uses her
favorite paint pens & glass paints to add
designs that enhance the holly-themed
cookies! Use your favorite holiday designs
to decorate a plain glass plate ⁓ just
along the edges, though, for food safety—
then let your friend know to handwash and dry the plate after every
morsel is gone!

*Bring out the holly...Holly Jolly Cookies that is! A sprinkling of green decorating
sugar and cinnamon candy "berries" make these cookies as pretty as they are
delicious. Give them on a hand-painted plate for added pizzazz.*

GINGERBREAD MAN CARD AND BAG

Place a gingerbread man cookie in a cellophane bag and tie closed with lengths of ribbons. For card, use spray adhesive (in a well-ventilated area) to glue a 4³/₄"x9¹/₂" piece of scrapbook paper to a same size piece of cardstock. Fold card in half.

For front of card, tear a 4¹/₂" square of scrapbook paper, use decorative-edge craft scissors to cut a 3³/₄" square of scrapbook paper, and tear a 3" square of fabric. Layer fabric and paper squares; attach to card using small brads. Adhere a dimensional sticker to center of card.

THE EASIEST GINGERBREAD MEN

A cake mix means this recipe is so simple, even the kids can make them!

18¹/₂-oz. pkg. spice cake mix
1 c. all-purpose flour
2 t. ground ginger
2 eggs
¹/₃ c. oil
¹/₂ c. molasses

Place cake mix, flour and ginger in a large mixing bowl; stir with a fork until blended. Mix in remaining ingredients. Beat with an electric mixer on medium speed for 2 minutes. Cover dough and refrigerate for 2 hours. Place dough on a floured surface; roll out to ¹/₄-inch thickness using a floured rolling pin. Cut out gingerbread people and place on greased baking sheets. Bake at 375 degrees for 8 to 10 minutes or until edges start to darken. Let cool on baking sheets for 5 minutes, then remove to wire racks to cool completely. Makes 1¹/₂ dozen.

Tanya Robinson
Ontario, Canada

Cookies are made of butter and love.

— NORWEGIAN PROVERB —

A holiday tradition just got a little easier! By using cake mix, you can create these munchable men in a snap. Drop one in a cellophane bag tied with a bow, then add a handmade card for a quick-to-fix gift.

Graham Cracker Brownies

★ a recipe from Peggy Duzik ★ Sioux City, IA

2 c. graham cracker crumbs
1 c. semi-sweet chocolate chips ★
1 t. baking powder
⅛ t. salt
14-oz. can sweetened
    condensed milk

(★ substitute mint chocolate chips
for a whole new taste!)

Combine all ingredients in a medium mixing bowl. Spread into a greased 8" x 8" baking pan. Bake at 350 degrees for 30 to 35 minutes or until a toothpick inserted near the center comes out clean. Cool on a wire rack and cut into squares. Makes 1½ dozen.

Fun Ideas!

This is an easy and yummy recipe to make with kids in the kitchen...

★ Let a little kid make the graham cracker crumbs ~ smash ★ smash ★ smash!

★ Kid-size aprons and potholders make chores pint-size.

★ Enjoy the finished product with a cold glass of milk!

GRANDMA'S MOLASSES POPCORN BALLS

My grandmother made these with my mom, and my mom made them every Christmas with me as a child. The best part was when the baking soda and butter were added...Mom said it was magic.

4 qts. popped popcorn
1 c. molasses
4 T. sugar
1 t. baking soda
1 t. butter

Place popcorn in a large bowl; set aside. Bring molasses and sugar to a boil in a large saucepan; boil for 20 minutes until mixture reaches the soft-ball stage, or 234 to 243 degrees on a candy thermometer. Remove from heat and quickly stir in baking soda and butter. Pour mixture over popcorn, stirring to coat. Grease hands with butter; shape popcorn into apple-size balls. Wrap individually in plastic wrap. Makes one to 2 dozen.

Cindy Hertz
Hummelstown, PA

OLD SOUTH POUND CAKE

If you thought the days were gone when pound cake really did take a pound of each ingredient...you were wrong!

1 lb. butter
1 lb. sugar
10 eggs, separated
1 lb. all-purpose flour
½ t. salt
1 t. lemon flavoring or
    vanilla extract

Cream butter; add sugar and beat well. In a separate bowl, beat egg yolks; add to creamed mixture.

Combine flour and salt; stir into creamed mixture. Add lemon flavoring or vanilla. Beat egg whites until stiff peaks form; fold into cake batter. Pour into a greased Bundt® pan. Bake at 300 degrees for 1½ hours. Serves 10 to 12.

Delinda Blakney
Bridgeview, IL

"Sharing food with another human being is an intimate act that should not be indulged in lightly."
— M.F.K. Fisher

CINNAMON CAKE

Inside each slice, you'll find sweet swirls of cinnamon.

18¼-oz. pkg. yellow cake mix
3.4-oz. pkg. instant vanilla
    pudding mix
¾ c. oil
¾ c. water
1 t. vanilla extract
½ t. butter flavoring
4 eggs
¼ c. sugar
1¼ t. cinnamon

Combine first 6 ingredients in a large mixing bowl. Beat in eggs, one at a time, until mixture is smooth; set aside. In a separate bowl, combine sugar and cinnamon. Grease a Bundt® pan and sprinkle with half the cinnamon-sugar mixture. Pour half the cake batter in pan; sprinkle remaining cinnamon-sugar mix on top. Pour remaining batter on top. Bake at 350 degrees for one hour or until golden. Allow cake to cool for several minutes before removing from pan; pour icing over top while still warm. Serves 10 to 12.

Icing:
1 c. powdered sugar
3 T. milk
¼ t. butter flavoring

Mix all ingredients until smooth.

L. Santa Ana
Lomita, CA

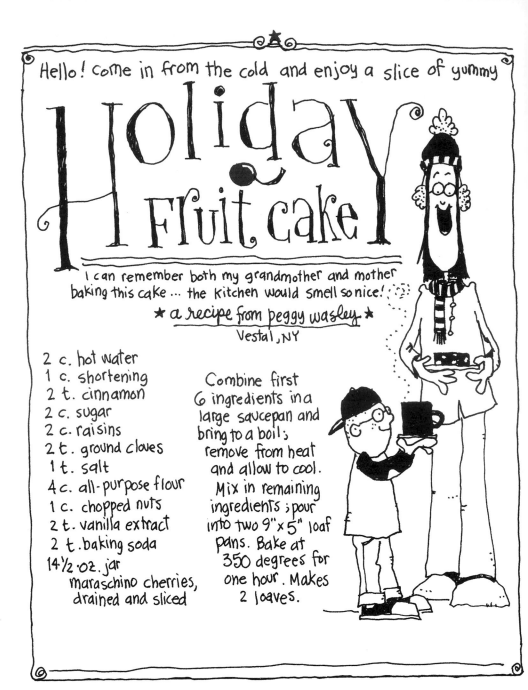

Hello! come in from the cold and enjoy a slice of yummy

Holiday Fruit cake

I can remember both my grandmother and mother baking this cake ... the kitchen would smell so nice!

★ *a recipe from peggy wasley* ★
Vestal, NY

2 c. hot water
1 c. shortening
2 t. cinnamon
2 c. sugar
2 c. raisins
2 t. ground cloves
1 t. salt
4 c. all-purpose flour
1 c. chopped nuts
2 t. vanilla extract
2 t. baking soda
14½-oz. jar
    maraschino cherries,
    drained and sliced

Combine first 6 ingredients in a large saucepan and bring to a boil; remove from heat and allow to cool. Mix in remaining ingredients; pour into two 9" x 5" loaf pans. Bake at 350 degrees for one hour. Makes 2 loaves.

Need a gift in a flurry? Line a clean, new one-gallon paint can with a tea towel, glue homemade paper snowflakes on the outside and then fill to the rim with homemade cookies. Wrap it all up in cellophane and tie with a homespun bow.

Trim a tea party tree...tie dainty teacups to the ends of branches, gather lacy hankies and clip onto tree using vintage costume jewelry pins. Dangling teaspoons and tea caddies add even more charm and sparkle.

Stir up a batch of Sugar-Dusted Pecan Squares to satisfy the sweet tooth on your Christmas list. The nutty-sweet goodness will be a much appreciated treat.

SUGAR-DUSTED PECAN SQUARES

Be sure to include these at your Christmas cookie exchange!

2 c. brown sugar, packed
1/2 c. plus 2 T. all-purpose flour
1/4 t. baking soda
2 c. chopped pecans
4 eggs
4 T. butter, melted
2 t. vanilla extract
Garnish: powdered sugar

Line a 9"X13" baking pan with aluminum foil, extending foil over ends of pan; grease foil. Mix together brown sugar, flour, baking soda and pecans in a small bowl; set aside. In a separate bowl, beat eggs; stir in melted butter. Stir in brown sugar mixture and vanilla. Pour mixture in pan; do not stir. Bake at 350 degrees for 20 minutes. Cool in pan on a wire rack. Use ends of foil to lift from pan. Cut into squares. Sprinkle lightly with powdered sugar. Makes 2 dozen.

Tamara Lucas
Guysville, OH

*S*tar light, star bright. Place a well greased star-shaped open cookie cutter on a greased aluminum foil-lined baking sheet. Fill with coarsely chopped peppermint candies and bake at 325 degrees until candy melts. Gently push out of form...pretty swirled candy stars!

Kate's Wooden Treat Basket

Paint a wooden basket RED. Tie a short length of silk ribbon through each end of a CHRISTMAS charm and glue to front of basket. For "TREATS" tags, CUT rectangles of green cardstock slightly larger than your alphabet charms, and rectangles of dark green cardstock larger than the green ones. Layer and GLUE rectangles together. Center a charm on each rectangle; punch a hole in paper through hole in the charm. Attach a jump ring through holes in each charm and rectangle. Thread tags onto a length of jute; wrap and knot around basket, spacing tags evenly.

Now line the basket with a festive piece of homespun... and you're all done!

Flavors of the Season

Oh, the happiness of Christmas
...all our loved ones gathered together,
the aroma of roasted turkey, savory side
dishes and sweet pies. Perhaps the only
thing more wonderful than sharing holiday
foods is the laughter that follows the
dishes around the table. These recipes for
fabulous feasts and yummy treats will help
spread the joy throughout your holidays.

*Herb-Roasted Turkey tastes fabulous, and it looks so festive when
surrounded by lady apples, orange slices and fresh herbs!*

good friends good food

_Christmas and friendship…each are good,
but together they're better! Share these tempting
dishes with the special people in your life
or ask a friend to join you in the kitchen.
The laughter will add its own special seasoning!_

HERB-ROASTED TURKEY

_A terrific turkey for dinner and for
sandwiches the day after._

14-lb. turkey
1 T. salt
1 t. pepper
18 sprigs fresh thyme, divided
4 onions, peeled and sliced
1 lb. leek, chopped
2 carrots, chopped
4 stalks celery, chopped
3 bay leaves
1 T. peppercorns
1½ c. butter, melted
1 t. fresh sage, chopped
1 t. fresh thyme, chopped
1 t. fresh chives, chopped

Carefully rinse and dry turkey inside and out; set aside giblets. Rub all surfaces with salt and pepper, including cavity. Insert meat thermometer into thickest part of thigh without touching bone. Place 12 sprigs of thyme inside turkey. Place vegetables, bay leaves, remaining thyme sprigs, peppercorns and giblets in bottom of large, heavy roasting pan. Place turkey on top of vegetables. Cover opening of cavity with aluminum foil. Brush butter over all surfaces of turkey; sprinkle with sage, thyme and chives. Cover loosely with tent of aluminum foil. Roast at 350 degrees for 2½ hours, undisturbed; remove aluminum foil to let skin brown. Roast and baste every 20 minutes for an additional hour and 15 minutes or until an internal temperature of 180 degrees is reached. Remove from oven. Transfer to platter and cover with aluminum foil; pan juices may be reserved for making gravy. Let turkey rest 15 to 20 minutes before carving. Serves 12 to 14.

Jo Ann
Gooseberry Patch

Herb-Roasted Turkey, Fresh Cranberry Relish, Feta & Walnut Salad

Everybody knows a turkey and some mistletoe
help to make the season bright. ∾ Mel Torme & Robert Wells

FRESH CRANBERRY RELISH

I make this simple recipe every Thanksgiving and Christmas at the request of my dad and husband. It nicely complements all the holiday favorites…turkey, ham, pork roast and stuffed winter squash. I like to garnish it with stars cut from the orange peel with a small cookie cutter.

12-oz. pkg. cranberries
2 apples, cored, peeled and
   quartered
2 pears, cored, peeled and
   quartered
2 oranges, peeled and sectioned
1/2 c. coarsely chopped pecans,
   optional
orange zest to taste
3/4 c. honey or to taste

Coarsely chop the fruit with a food processor. Mix in nuts and orange zest; sweeten to taste with honey. Turn into a serving dish. Makes about 8 cups.

Karen Healey
Rutland, MA

FETA & WALNUT SALAD

If I think my guests won't care for the tart taste of cranberries, I just substitute cherry tomatoes.

5-oz. pkg. mixed salad greens
3/4 c. dried cranberries
1/2 c. feta cheese, crumbled
1/2 c. chopped walnuts, toasted
2 T. balsamic vinegar
1 T. honey
1 t. Dijon mustard
1/4 c. olive oil

Toss greens, cranberries, feta cheese and walnuts together in a large bowl. In a small bowl, whisk vinegar and honey until well blended; gradually add oil, whisking until combined. Pour over salad and toss to coat. Serves 4 to 6.

Denise Neal
Clayton, CA

AMBROSIA

Mom made this 5-cup salad in the 1950's and it's still popular today!

1 T. sugar
1 c. sour cream
1 c. miniature marshmallows
1 c. crushed pineapple, drained
1 c. flaked coconut
1 c. mandarin oranges, drained
Garnish: maraschino cherries
   (optional)

Stir sugar into sour cream; add remaining ingredients. Stir well; chill. Garnish before serving, if desired. Makes 5 cups.

Mary Ann Nemecek
Springfield, IL

"Remember, no man is a failure who has friends."

— Clarence the Angel,
It's a Wonderful Life

Ambrosia

Need a Quick Centerpiece for your holiday table?

Wrap different-size boxes, stack them into a tower and glue on inexpensive ornaments where you can.

Green Bean-Corn Casserole

GREEN BEAN-CORN CASSEROLE

Try this quick & easy side dish. It's a terrific change from the more traditional green bean casseroles.

14^1/$_2$-oz. can French-style green
    beans, drained
15^1/$_4$-oz. can corn, drained
1 c. shredded sharp Cheddar cheese
^{1}/$_2$ c. onion, chopped
1 c. sour cream
8-oz. can sliced water chestnuts,
    drained
10^3/$_4$-oz. can cream of celery soup
^{1}/$_2$ c. butter, melted
1 sleeve round buttery crackers,
    crushed

Spread green beans on the bottom of an ungreased 13"x9" baking pan; layer corn on top. In a separate bowl, mix cheese, onion, sour cream, water chestnuts and celery soup together; spread over the vegetables. Combine butter and crackers; sprinkle on top. Bake at 400 degrees for 40 minutes or until golden. Serves 6.

Jennifer Thomas
Coffeyville, KS

CORNBREAD STUFFING

Mound stuffing on a large platter and top with a baked turkey breast...add teaspoonfuls of cranberry sauce evenly spaced around the rim for a meal that's pretty and filling.

16-oz. pkg. cornbread stuffing mix
3 c. water
^{1}/$_2$ c. butter, divided
1 c. onion, chopped
1 c. celery, chopped
1 c. ground Italian sausage,
    browned and crumbled
1 c. sweetened, dried cranberries
^{1}/$_2$ c. chopped pecans

Prepare stuffing according to package directions using 3 cups water and ^{1}/$_4$ cup butter; set aside. Sauté the onion and celery in remaining butter until translucent. Stir onion, celery, sausage, cranberries and pecans into stuffing; toss well to coat. Spread in a lightly greased 13"x9" baking pan; bake at 350 degrees for 30 minutes. Makes about 12 cups.

Kathy Grashoff
Fort Wayne, IN

*P*lay holiday music quietly during family dinners...try jazz, contemporary and country themes, and find your family's favorites.

A row of red apples tucked into pine boughs arranged down the middle of the table offers guests a simple country welcome.

SUNDAY DINNER POTATO ROLLS

Growing up, Sunday dinner was the most important meal in our home, and these rolls were always served fresh from the oven.

2 pkgs. active dry yeast
2 c. warm water
1/2 c. sugar
1 1/4 T. salt
1 c. warm mashed potatoes
1/2 c. butter, softened
2 eggs
7 1/2 c. all-purpose flour, divided
3 T. butter, melted

Dissolve yeast in water; add sugar, salt, potatoes, butter and eggs. Gradually beat in 3 1/2 cups flour; continue beating for 2 minutes. Mix in remaining flour; knead dough several strokes. Coat dough with melted butter; place in a bowl and refrigerate 2 hours. Punch down; refrigerate overnight. Punch down and knead. Divide dough in half; shape each half into 24 rolls. Place rolls on lightly greased baking sheets; let dough rise in a warm place. Bake at 325 degrees for 40 minutes. Makes 4 dozen rolls.

Mary Murray
Gooseberry Patch

"Peace on earth will come to stay, when we live Christmas every day."
— Helen Steiner Rice

"To get the full value of joy, you must have someone to divide it with."
— Mark Twain

CARAMEL PECAN PIE ...ooey. Gooey and unbearably GOOD!

36 CARAMELS, UNWRAPPED
1/4 c. BUTTER
1/4 c. MILK
3/4 c. SUGAR
3 EGGS
1/2 t. VANILLA EXTRACT
1/4 t. SALT
1 c. PECAN HALVES
9-INCH PIE CRUST

COMBINE CARAMELS, BUTTER & MILK IN HEAVY SAUCEPAN; HEAT UNTIL MELTED & CREAMY, STIRRING OFTEN. REMOVE FROM HEAT; SET ASIDE. BLEND SUGAR, EGGS & VANILLA & SALT TOGETHER; GRADUALLY MIX IN CARAMEL MIXTURE. FOLD IN PECANS; SPREAD IN PIE CRUST. BAKE AT 350 DEGREES FOR 45 TO 50 MINUTES; COOL 'TIL FIRM. SERVES 8.

JOAN BROCHU
HARDWICK, VT

Caramel Pecan Pie

This selection of yummy appetizers, hearty entrées and oh-so-good sweets will secure your title as Hostess with the Mostest! And the wide range of flavors will have your guests peeking in the kitchen to see what wonderful dish is coming their way next. They'll never guess that each delicious recipe only uses a few ingredients!

Blue Cheese-Onion Cheese Ball

SEASONED OYSTER CRACKERS

So good to snack on by themselves or sprinkled into homemade soups and stews.

1½ c. oil
2 1-oz. pkgs. ranch seasoning and
　　salad dressing mix
1 T. lemon pepper
1 T. dill weed
2 10-oz. pkgs. oyster crackers

Whisk first 4 ingredients together; pour over oyster crackers. Toss gently; spread on an ungreased baking sheet. Bake at 225 degrees for one hour, stirring every 15 minutes. Store in an airtight container. Makes 24 servings.

Jen Sell
Farmington, MN

BLUE CHEESE-ONION CHEESE BALL

Serve with crackers, veggies or bagel chips.

8-oz. pkg. cream cheese, softened
4-oz. pkg. crumbled blue cheese
¼ c. green olives, diced
¼ c. onion, diced
¾ c. chopped walnuts

Combine first 4 ingredients; mix well. Form into a round ball; roll in walnuts until covered. Serves 6 to 8.

Tricia Battersby
Woodhaven, MI

SIZZLING SALSA DIP

If you like it hot, this is the dip for you...try it once and you'll be addicted.

1 lb. hot Italian ground sausage,
　　browned
16-oz. jar hot salsa
16-oz. pkg. pasteurized process
　　mild Mexican cheese spread,
　　cubed

Combine ingredients in a slow cooker; heat on low setting until cheese melts, stirring frequently. Makes about 3½ cups.

Debbie Sundermeier
Brunswick, OH

Spunky Spinach Dip

SPUNKY SPINACH DIP

Whether served with colorful tortilla chips, fresh veggies or bread cubes, it's irresistible.

2 c. salsa
2 c. shredded Monterey Jack
    cheese
8-oz. pkg. cream cheese, softened
    and cubed
10-oz. pkg. frozen chopped
    spinach, thawed and drained
1 c. pitted black olives, chopped

Mix all ingredients together; stir well. Place in a microwave-safe bowl; microwave on medium setting until heated through. Serves about 10.

Beverly Weppler
Atlantic, IA

CHEESE BREAD BITES

I like simple and easy make-ahead recipes. This is a favorite of my grandchildren and family. When they tell me when they're flying into Florida, I start making and storing these right away!

1 loaf French bread, crusts trimmed
1 c. butter
¹/₂ lb. sharp Cheddar cheese,
    cubed
2 3-oz. pkgs. cream cheese,
    softened
4 egg whites, stiffly beaten

Cube bread; set aside. Melt butter and cheeses in a double boiler over low heat, stirring often. Remove from heat; fold in egg whites. Dip bread cubes into cheese mixture; set on greased baking sheets. Place in freezer until frozen; remove from baking sheets and store in plastic zipping bags in the freezer. To serve, bake frozen bites at 400 degrees for 12 minutes on greased baking sheets. Serves 8 to 10.

Nola Laflin
Coral Springs, FL

TAMALE PIE

Ready-made tamales make this pie oh-so quick.

15-oz. can chili, divided
10-oz. pkg. corn chips, divided
1 onion, minced and divided
2 13½-oz. cans beef tamales,
    chopped and divided
2 c. shredded Cheddar cheese,
    divided

Spread one cup chili in the bottom of a greased 2-quart casserole dish; layer half the corn chips, half the onion and one can tamales on top. Sprinkle with half the cheese; repeat layers. Cover and bake at 350 degrees for one hour. Let cool for 10 minutes before serving. Makes 12 servings.

Kelly Cook
Dunedin, FL

the decision to have a child is to accept that your ♥heart♥ will forever walk about outside your body. ~ K. HADLEY

Pepper-Onion Steak Sauté

PEPPER-ONION STEAK SAUTÉ

Spoon on top of grilled ribeye steaks right before serving.

1 onion, sliced
1 green pepper, sliced
1 red pepper, sliced
8-oz. pkg. sliced mushrooms
2 T. butter
minced garlic to taste

Sauté ingredients together until tender. Makes 4 servings.

Barb Jones
Fort Dodge, IA

PECAN CHICKEN

Garnish with a pecan half, if desired.

4 boneless, skinless chicken
    breasts
2 T. honey
2 T. Dijon mustard
2 T. ground pecans

Place chicken between 2 sheets of heavy-duty plastic wrap; flatten to ¼-inch thickness using a rolling pin. Set aside. Mix honey and mustard together; spread over chicken. Coat chicken with pecans; arrange in a lightly greased 13" x 9" baking pan. Bake at 350 degrees for 15 to 18 minutes. Makes 4 servings.

Linda Wiist
Duluth, GA

Heavenly 'Beefy Taco Soup

a recipe from
ERIN McRAE
★ Beaverton, OR ★

Top each bowl with a halo of sour cream, chopped green onion and a sprinkle of shredded cheese!

1 LB. GROUND BEEF, BROWNED
14.½ OZ. CAN STEWED TOMATOES
15. OZ. CAN KIDNEY BEANS,
    RINSED and DRAINED
1.¼.OZ. PKG. TACO SEASONING MIX
8.OZ. CAN TOMATO SAUCE

★

Brown beef in a large skillet; drain. Stir in tomatoes and remaining ingredients; pour into a slow cooker. Heat on low setting for 6 to 8 hours; stir occasionally. Add water to thin consistency as desired. Makes 4 to 6 servings.

Beefy Taco Soup

CHEESY HASHBROWNS

Top with French fried onions for added crunch, if you'd like.

30-oz. pkg. frozen shredded
    hashbrowns, thawed
2 c. sour cream
2 10³/₄-oz. cans cream of
    mushroom soup
1 onion, chopped
2 to 3 c. shredded Cheddar
    cheese, divided

Combine hashbrowns, sour cream, soup, onion and 2 cups cheese together; mix well. Spread into a lightly buttered 13"x9" baking dish; sprinkle with remaining cheese. Bake at 350 degrees for one hour. Makes 8 to 10 servings.

Joanne McDonald
British Colombia, Canada

Ho-Ho-Ho! Invite a local Santa to drop in during this year's family get-together. What a joy for all ages!

BAKED FRENCH ONION RICE

This simple, tasty dish requires very little prep time.

1 c. long-cooking rice, uncooked
14½-oz. can beef broth
10½-oz. can French onion soup
4-oz. can mushroom stems and
    pieces, drained
¼ c. margarine

Place rice into an ungreased 2-quart casserole dish; add beef broth, soup and mushroom pieces, stirring well. Dot with margarine; cover and bake at 350 degrees for 50 minutes. Makes 4 servings.

Tammie McClendon
Guild, TN

Nostalgic holiday postcards make charming placecards. Punch 2 holes in the top, string with thin velvet ribbon, tie on a pair of jingle bells and loop around dining room chair backs.

Simple Broccoli Casserole

Mix in shredded, cooked chicken if you like!

10·oz. pkg. frozen broccoli, thawed
10¾·oz. can cream of chicken soup
10¾·oz. can cream of mushroom soup
6·oz. pkg. herb·flavored stuffing mix
½ c. butter, melted

*

Place broccoli and soups in a buttered 1·½ quart casserole dish; mix well. Toss stuffing with butter in a mixing bowl; add to casserole dish. Stir gently to mix. Bake at 350 degrees for 40 to 45 minutes. Makes 4 to 6 servings.

~Margie Schaffner~
Altoona, IA

Simple Broccoli Casserole

LEMONY POPPY SEED BREAD

Mini loaves wrapped in pretty plastic wrap make welcome gifts any time of the year.

18¼-oz. pkg. lemon cake mix
3.4-oz. pkg. instant lemon
    pudding mix
4 eggs
1 c. water
½ c. oil
1 to 2 t. poppy seed

Blend first 5 ingredients together, mixing well. Stir in poppy seeds. Pour into two, 8"x4" lightly greased and floured loaf pans; bake at 350 degrees for 45 minutes. Cool in pans 10 minutes. Makes 16 servings.

Vicki Moats
Wyoming, IL

If you have extra garland left over from decorating the tree, use it to decorate your holiday table! Wind it around the base of your centerpiece, or cut it apart to place around each plate. Fast & fun!

ROCKY ROAD BITES

It's hard to eat just one!

2 lbs. melting chocolate, melted
1 c. chopped pecans, toasted
10½-oz. bag mini marshmallows

Mix ingredients together; spread on an aluminum foil-lined baking sheet. Let set for one hour; break into bite-size pieces. Makes 18 servings.

Ann Aiken
Spicewood, TX

A quick & easy table topper! Place photos of previous Christmas get-togethers under clear plastic place mats. Everyone will have fun reminiscing at dinner.

Lemony Poppy Seed Bread

CHOCOLATE marshmallow PIE

I received this recipe from a dear friend who's 90 years old... we make this dessert often and enjoy it!

16 regular size marshmallows
4 1.45-oz. milk chocolate candy bars with almonds
½ c. milk
8-oz. carton whipping cream
9-inch graham cracker pie crust (homemade)

Heat marshmallows, candy bars & milk in a double boiler 'til marshmallows & chocolate melt; stir often. Remove from heat; stir in whipping cream. Pour into pie crust; refrigerate 'til firm. Serves 8.

~ Brenda Neal ~

★ Taneyville, MO

97

They'll Never Know It's Not Homemade!

The recipe for "seasoned" greetings begins in the kitchen with this festive array of soon-to-be holiday favorites! Even Kate can whip up these yummy dishes, because they all feature ready-made foods from the grocery store. So, with just a pinch of work, you'll have a pound of wonderful treasures!

HERBED FAN DINNER ROLLS

When baked, the layers of the roll spread out to mimic a fan.

¼ c. butter or margarine, melted
½ t. dried Italian seasoning
11-oz. pkg. refrigerated loaf bread

Combine butter and Italian seasoning, stirring well. Roll dough into a 13" square. Cut into four equal strips. Stack strips on top of each other. Cut strips crosswise into 6 equal pieces. Place each piece, cut side up, into greased muffin pan; brush with butter mixture. Cover and let rise in a warm place (85 degrees), free from drafts, 25 minutes or until doubled in bulk. Bake at 375 degrees for 22 to 25 minutes or until golden. Brush with butter mixture again, if desired. Makes 6.

Make-Ahead: Place dough pieces in muffin pan; brush with butter mixture. Cover and freeze. Thaw, covered in a warm place 2 hours or until doubled in bulk. Bake as directed.

ITALIAN CHEESE TERRINE

Have provolone cheese and salami thinly sliced at a deli. Packaged, pre-sliced cheese and salami are too thick for this recipe.

1 lb. thinly sliced provolone cheese
2¾-oz. jar pesto sauce
¾ lb. thinly sliced salami
3 T. commercial Italian salad dressing
Garnish: fresh thyme sprigs
marinara or pasta sauce

Place one slice of cheese on a large piece of heavy-duty plastic wrap; spread one teaspoon of pesto over cheese. Top with 3 slices of salami. (Do not stack salami.) Brush salami lightly with salad dressing. Repeat layers, using all of cheese, pesto, salami, and salad dressing, and ending with cheese. Surround stack with a few sprigs of thyme, if desired. Fold plastic wrap over layers, sealing securely. Place a heavy object, such as a small cast-iron skillet, on top of cheese terrine. Cover and chill at least 24 hours or up to 3 days. Remove plastic wrap to serve terrine. Cut into wedges, using an electric knife or sharp knife. Serve with breadsticks, crackers, and desired sauce. Makes about 12 appetizer servings.

Herbed Fan Dinner Rolls

sweet treats

Quick 'n Easy Pie

WALNUT CRANBERRY SAUCE

A hint of cinnamon, splash of dark vinegar and handful of toasted nuts make this cranberry sauce worthy of gift giving. Deliver it in a jar tied with ribbon.

16-oz. can whole-berry cranberry
    sauce
$1/3$ c. strawberry preserves
$1^1/2$ T. sugar
$1/4$ t. cinnamon
$1/2$ c. coarsely chopped walnuts,
    toasted
1 T. balsamic vinegar or red wine
    such as Pinot Noir

Combine first 4 ingredients in a saucepan. Cook over medium heat, stirring often, just until thoroughly heated. Remove from heat; stir in walnuts and vinegar. Cover and chill until ready to serve. Serve with turkey or ham. Makes $2^1/4$ cups.

QUICK 'N EASY PIE

This pie will vanish so fast...you'd better make two!

1 qt. vanilla ice cream, softened
6-oz. chocolate cookie crumb
    crust
$14^1/2$-oz. jar milk chocolate ice
    cream topping
3 1.4-oz. English toffee candy
    bars, chopped

Spread vanilla ice cream in crumb crust. Cover and freeze until ice cream is firm. Spread ice cream topping over ice cream; sprinkle with chopped candy, and freeze until firm. Serve immediately.

Sugar-n-spice makes everything nice.

— Old Saying

Snowball Sandwich Cookies

Little fingers will enjoy dipping these cookies in melted chocolate!

6-oz. pkg. white
   chocolate, chopped

2 12-oz. boxes Danish
   wedding cookies

Melt white chocolate in a heavy saucepan over low heat, stirring occasionally. Dip flat sides of half the cookies in white chocolate, and top with flat sides of remaining cookies. Let stand until white chocolate is firm. Makes 4 dozen.

99

HALF DIP TIPS

Make store-bought chocolate cookies more irresistible with even more chocolate! Here are some ideas worth dipping into.

Biscotti:

Melt 12 ounces chocolate candy coating or semisweet chocolate in top of a double boiler over hot water. Remove from heat. Fill a large mug with melted chocolate coating. Dip biscotti halfway into coating. Shake off excess coating and let dry on wax paper over a wire rack. Refill mug as needed.

Chocolate Snaps:

Follow procedure above, only using 10 ounces vanilla candy coating or white baking bars.

Dipped Cookies:

Place one cup milk chocolate morsels in a 2-cup glass measure. Microwave at HIGH one to 2 minutes or until melted, stirring every 30 seconds. Dip 20 cookies halfway into chocolate. Let dry on wax paper over wire racks. Repeat with another one cup morsels and remaining cookies. (It takes about 2 hours for milk chocolate coating to dry.)

Dipped and Drizzled Cookies:

Dip cookies as previously directed. Then seal ½ cup chocolate or vanilla morsels in a heavy-duty, plastic zipping bag. Dip bag in very hot water 2 to 3 minutes or until chocolate melts. Remove bag from water; snip a tiny hole in one corner of bag. Drizzle chocolate over dipped cookies.

Dipped and Drizzled Fruit:

Dip various fruits such as fresh strawberries or dried apricots in melted semi-sweet chocolate. Let dry on wax paper-lined trays. Or drizzle fruit, if desired, as directed above.

Speedy Sorbet

SPEEDY SORBET

What a fun way to eat fruit!

2 21-oz. cans blueberry or cherry pie filling

Freeze unopened cans of pie filling until frozen solid, at least 18 hours or up to one month. Submerge unopened cans in hot water one to 2 minutes. Open both ends of cans, and slide frozen mixture into a bowl. Break into chunks. Position knife blade in food processor bowl; add chunks. Process until smooth, stopping as necessary to scrape down sides. Pour fruit mixture into an 8"x8" baking pan. Freeze until firm. Let stand 10 minutes before serving. Makes 6 servings.

Pineapple Sorbet: Substitute two 20-oz. cans chunk pineapple in heavy syrup for pie filling.

Strawberry Sorbet: Substitute three 10-oz. packages frozen strawberries in syrup for pie filling.

CHOCOLATE MINT TORTE

Serve this refrigerated or frozen...it's delectable either way.

17-oz. loaf marble pound cake
1/4 c. plus 2 T. chocolate syrup, divided
4.67-oz. pkg. chocolate-covered mint wafer candies, divided
2 c. whipping cream, divided
1/2 c. sifted powdered sugar, divided

Slice pound cake in half horizontally; slice each half in half again horizontally. Brush top of each layer with 1 1/2 tablespoons chocolate syrup; let stand 15 minutes for layers to absorb syrup. Reserve 8 whole candies for garnish. Finely chop remaining candies. Combine one cup whipping cream and 1/4 cup powdered sugar in a large mixing bowl; beat at high speed with an electric mixer until stiff peaks form. Fold chopped candies into sweetened whipped cream. Place one cake layer on a serving plate; spread 1/2 cup whipped cream mixture on cake layer. Repeat procedure with next 2 cake layers, stacking layers. Top with remaining cake layer and freeze until firm. Beat remaining whipping cream and remaining powdered sugar together. Frost top and sides of torte with mixture. Cover and chill or freeze until ready to serve or up to 8 hours. Pull a vegetable peeler down sides of reserved 8 candies to make tiny shavings. Sprinkle candy shavings over torte before serving. Makes one 9" torte.

Chocolate Mint Torte

LEMON FONDUE

Whereas melted chocolate is typically blended with cream and liqueur, we've concocted a luscious lemon version of the popular dessert fondue. Pears and gingersnaps are a must for dipping.

11 1/4-oz. jar lemon curd
1/3 c. sweetened condensed milk
1/4 c. half-and-half
Garnish: lemon zest

Combine first 3 ingredients in a small bowl, and stir well. Spoon into a footed serving dish. Serve with fresh fruit, gingersnap, and pound cake cubes. Garnish dish, if desired. Makes 2 cups.

Give kazoos as party favors, then everyone can play along with the Christmas music.

Make A Joyful noise!

cook slow, save Time!

There's just something magical about a meal from a slow cooker. All those wonderful flavors mingling gently together produce meats that are more tender, and broths & sauces that seem more robust. And while your favorite dishes slowly simmer, you're free to make good use of the time you would otherwise have spent in the kitchen!

Tried & True Meat Loaf

TRIED & TRUE MEAT LOAF

Save any leftovers for tasty meatloaf sandwiches.

1¹/₂ lbs. ground beef
³/₄ c. bread crumbs
2 eggs
³/₄ c. milk
1 onion, chopped
1 t. salt
¹/₄ t. pepper
¹/₄ c. catsup
2 T. brown sugar, packed
1 t. dry mustard
¹/₄ t. nutmeg

Combine beef, bread crumbs, eggs, milk, onion, salt and pepper; form mixture into a loaf. Place in a slow cooker; heat on high setting one hour. Reduce to low setting and cook 4 to 5 hours. Whisk remaining ingredients together; pour over beef. Heat on high setting an additional 15 minutes. Serves 4 to 6.

Take a child to the grocery store to help choose dinner ingredients with all the fixings to drop off at a local food pantry...a tradition well worth keeping.

SHREDDED BEEF BBQ

A family favorite.

2³/₄-lb. beef chuck roast
1 onion, sliced
½ c. water
½ c. plus 1 T. brown sugar, packed
    and divided
1 T. vinegar
2 t. lemon juice
7-oz. bottle catsup
¼ t. salt
1½ t. Worcestershire sauce
½ t. dried mustard
pepper to taste

Place roast in a 2-quart slow cooker; add enough water to cover. Top with onion; heat on high setting for one hour. Reduce to low setting and cook 7 hours. Shred roast with 2 forks; place in a 10" skillet. Add ½ cup water; bring to a boil. Stir in ½ cup brown sugar; heat until liquid evaporates. Combine remaining ingredients with remaining brown sugar in a mixing bowl; pour over beef mixture. Heat until warmed through. Serves 6.

LANDSLIDE FRENCH DIP

Put ingredients in the slow cooker before leaving in the morning and dinner's ready when you come home!

3-lb. rump roast
1 cube beef bouillon
3 to 4 peppercorns
½ c. soy sauce
1 bay leaf
1 t. garlic powder

Place roast in a slow cooker; add remaining ingredients. Pour in enough water to cover the roast; heat on high setting for one hour. Reduce to low setting and cook 9 hours. Remove and discard bay leaf before serving. Serves 6.

Shredded Beef BBQ

*SLOW * COOKER*
Smothered * Steak

⅓ c. all-purpose flour
1 t. garlic salt
½ t. pepper
1½ lbs. round steak,
    cut into strips
1 onion, sliced
2 green peppers, sliced
4-oz. can sliced mushrooms,
    drained
10-oz. pkg. frozen
french-style green beans
¼ c. soy sauce
9 c. prepared white rice

Add first 3 ingredients to a one-gallon plastic zipping bag; shake to mix. Place steak strips in bag; shake to coat. Arrange steak in a slow cooker; layer onion, green peppers, mushrooms & green beans on top. Pour soy sauce over top; heat on high setting for one hour. Reduce heat to low and heat for 8 hours; serve on bed of warm rice. Serves 6.

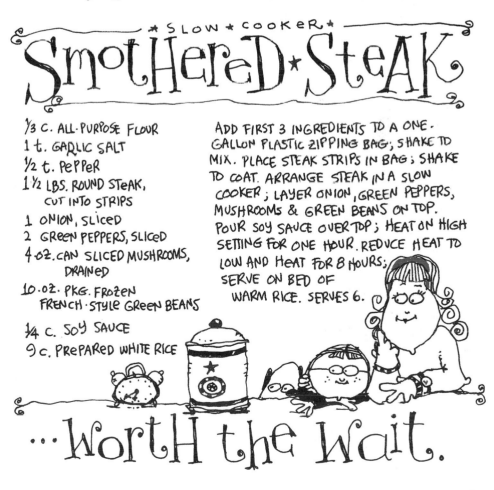

...worth the wait.

Jalapeño-Chicken Chili

JALAPEÑO-CHICKEN CHILI

Jalapeño peppers and salsa spice up this chili.

2 c. chicken, cooked and cubed
4 15-oz. cans Great Northern
    beans
1 onion, chopped
$^1/_2$ c. red pepper, diced
$^1/_2$ c. green pepper, diced
2 jalapeño peppers, finely diced
2 cloves garlic, minced
$1^1/_2$ t. cumin
$^1/_2$ t. dried oregano

$^3/_4$ t. salt
$^1/_4$ c. water
$^1/_2$ t. chicken bouillon granules
1 to 2 c. salsa

Stir all ingredients except salsa together; spoon into a slow cooker. Heat on high setting for 5 hours, or cook on high setting one hour and reduce to low setting and cook 7 to 9 hours; stir occasionally. Add salsa during last hour of heating. Serves 4 to 6.

ARTICHOKE-CHICKEN PASTA

So easy to make and so yummy!

16-oz. frozen grilled chicken
    breast strips
1 T. chicken bouillon granules
$^1/_4$ c. water
17-oz. jar alfredo sauce
$6^1/_2$-oz. jar marinated artichoke
    hearts, drained
6-oz. pkg. angel hair pasta, cooked

Place chicken strips in a 4-quart slow cooker with bouillon and water. Cook on low for 2 to 3 hours. One half hour prior to serving, turn cooker to high and place sauce and artichokes over chicken. Serve over pasta. Makes 4 servings.

Mary Luinstra
Great Falls, MT

CHOW-DOWN
CORN CHOWDER

Hearty and delicious.

6 slices bacon, diced
$^1/_2$ c. onion, chopped
2 c. potatoes, peeled & diced
2 10-oz. pkgs. frozen
    whole-kernel corn
16-oz. can cream-style corn
$1^1/_4$ T. sugar
$1^1/_2$ t. Worcestershire sauce
$1^1/_4$ t. seasoned salt
$^1/_2$ t. pepper
1 c. water

In skillet, fry bacon until crisp. Remove bacon; reserve drippings. Add onion and potatoes to drippings and sauté for about 5 minutes; drain well. Combine all ingredients in a $3^1/_2$-quart slow cooker; stir well. Cover and cook on low for 4 to 7 hours. Makes 4 servings.

Marian Buckley
Fontana, CA

Try serving chili and chowder in bread bowls...yummy! Scoop out bread rounds and brush the insides with olive oil or corn oil. Bake in a 350-degree oven for 10 minutes, then fill with soup.

Good things come to those who wait.

Mom's Spaghetti Sauce

1 onion, diced
3 cloves garlic, chopped
1 T. butter
3 14½-oz. cans tomatoes
3 6-oz. cans tomato paste
2 c. water
¼ t. salt
½ t. pepper
½ t. dried basil
½ t. dried oregano
½ t. garlic powder
½ t. dried thyme
1 t. Italian seasoning
2 bay leaves
1 T. dried parsley

⅛ t. sugar
3 T. olive oil

Sauté onion and garlic in butter; set aside. Blend tomatoes and tomato paste in a blender until smooth; stir in onion and garlic. Pour into slow cooker; mix in remaining ingredients. Heat on high setting for approximately 3 hours, stirring occasionally; remove bay leaves before serving. Makes about 5 cups.

Everybody's Favorite!

Easy Potato Soup

EASY POTATO SOUP

This soup will warm you from the inside out.

4 to 5 potatoes, peeled and cubed
10¾-oz. can cream of celery soup
10¾-oz. can cream of chicken soup
1⅓ c. water
4⅔ c. milk
6.6-oz. pkg. instant mashed
    potato flakes
Garnish: bacon bits, green onions
    and shredded Cheddar cheese

Place potatoes, soups and water into a slow cooker; heat on high setting until potatoes are tender, about 2 to 3 hours. Add milk and instant mashed potatoes to reach desired consistency, stirring constantly. Heat 2 to 3 hours longer; spoon into bowls to serve. Top with garnishes. Serves 4 to 6.

GOOD HONEY-GARLIC CHICKEN WINGS

These delicious wings will be ready when the "big game" starts.

3 lbs. chicken wings,
    cleaned and halved
salt and pepper to taste
1 c. honey
1/2 c. soy sauce
2 T. oil
2 T. catsup
1 clove garlic, minced

Sprinkle chicken with salt and pepper. In a mixing bowl, combine remaining ingredients and mix well. Place chicken in a 4-quart slow cooker and pour sauce over. Cook on high for one hour. Reduce to low and cook 5 to 7 hours. Makes 8 to 12 servings.

Mary Murray
Gooseberry Patch

CHICKEN & GREEN BEAN BAKE

A full meal in one dish.

2 to 3 boneless, skinless chicken
    breasts
salt, pepper and garlic powder to
    taste
10³/₄-oz. can cream of mushroom
    soup
1/2 c. milk
14¹/₂-oz. can green beans, drained
2.8-oz. can French fried onions

Place chicken breasts in a slow cooker; season with salt, pepper and garlic powder. Heat until juices run clear when chicken is pierced with a fork, approximately 2 to 3 hours on high setting; drain. Add mushroom soup, milk and green beans; sprinkle top with French fried onions. Cover and heat 30 minutes longer. Serves 4.

POT ROAST & VEGGIES

Come home to a perfect dinner!

2 to 4-lb. pot roast
salt and pepper to taste
4 T. all-purpose flour
1/4 c. cold water
1 t. browning sauce
1 clove garlic, minced
2 onions, coarsely chopped
5 potatoes, peeled and coarsely
    chopped
3 carrots, coarsely chopped

Cut pot roast in half; place in a 4-quart slow cooker. Sprinkle with salt and pepper. Make a paste of flour and cold water; stir in browning sauce and spread over roast. Add garlic, onions, potatoes and carrots. Cover and cook on high setting for one hour. Reduce to low setting and cook 7 to 9 hours. Serves 4 to 6.

Donna Dye
London, OH

No longer
    forward nor behind
    I look in hope or fear;
But,
grateful,
    take the good I find,
The best of
now and
here.
-John Greenleaf Whittier-

Pot Roast & Veggies

CARAMEL PIE

They'll never believe you made it in a slow cooker!

2 14-ounce cans sweetened
   condensed milk
9-inch graham cracker pie crust
8-oz. container frozen whipped
   topping, thawed
1.4-oz. English toffee candy bar,
   coarsely chopped

Pour condensed milk into a 1-quart glass measuring cup; cover with foil. Place in a 3½-quart slow cooker, adding water around cup to milk level. Cook, covered, 8 to 9 hours or until mixture is the color of peanut butter; stir with a wire whisk. Pour into pie crust; chill one hour or until firm. Spread whipped topping over top of pie, and sprinkle evenly with chopped candy bar. Makes 6 to 8 servings.

Caramel Pie

MACARONI & CHEESE

An all-time favorite of kids everywhere.

7-oz. pkg. macaroni, cooked
12-oz. can evaporated milk
3 eggs, beaten
½ c. butter, melted
salt and pepper to taste
3 c. Cheddar cheese, grated
   and divided

Combine milk, eggs and butter, whisking until blended. Cook over medium heat, stirring constantly, until slightly thickened. Stir in macaroni, salt and pepper and 2 cups cheese; stir well. Pour into a 5-quart slow cooker and sprinkle with remaining cheese. Cover and cook on low for 3 hours. Do not take lid off until ready to serve. Makes 12 servings.

Stacie Seiders
Oakton, VA

"May peace and plenty be the first to lift the latch on your door, and happiness be guided to your home by the candle of Christmas!"
   — Irish Blessing

Prayer is the simplest form of speech that infant lips can try;
Prayer the sublimest strains that reach **The Majesty** on high.
~ James Montgomery ~

A CUP OF CHEER

A mug of Candy Cane Cocoa is just the thing to chase the chill after a day of building snowmen. Or maybe you need Apple-Cranberry Sparkler to help you cool down from a long evening of trimming the tree? Remember to make at least two servings for everyone, because these refreshments will disappear almost as fast as you can pour them.

Candy Cane Cocoa

CANDY CANE COCOA

This will warm you head-to-toe on those snowy nights.

4 c. milk
³/₄ c. sugar
1 t. peppermint extract
1¹/₂ c. baking cocoa
1 pt. mint chocolate chip
   ice cream
chocolate syrup
8 candy canes, crushed

Combine milk, sugar, peppermint extract and cocoa in a large saucepan. Heat over medium heat until hot; do not boil. Divide evenly into 8 large mugs. Float a scoop of ice cream in each mug; drizzle with chocolate syrup and sprinkle with candy cane pieces. Makes 8 servings.

Pat Ghann-Akers
Bayfield, CO

PINEAPPLE WASSAIL

Bring to a holiday open house while warm...mmmm.

4 c. unsweetened pineapple juice
12-oz. can apricot nectar
2 c. apple cider
1½ c. orange juice
2 3-inch cinnamon sticks
1 t. whole cloves
4 cardamom seeds, crushed

Combine ingredients in a 3-quart saucepan; heat to boiling. Reduce heat and simmer 15 to 20 minutes; strain into serving glasses or punch bowl. Serve warm. Makes about 2 quarts.

COMFY CIDER

Grab a mug of cider and snuggle down in front of the fireplace.

4 c. apple cider
2 c. cranberry juice
46-oz. can apricot nectar
1 c. orange juice
¾ c. sugar
2 3-inch cinnamon sticks
1 orange, peeled and sectioned

Place ingredients in a slow cooker; heat on low setting until warmed through, 4 to 6 hours. Strain before serving, discarding solids. Serves 10 to 12.

Add a bit of sparkle and spice to holiday drinks...tie a little ornament or bauble onto a cinnamon stick. The cinnamon stick is a great stirrer, while the ornament dangles over your mug of hot cocoa, mulled cider or creamy eggnog.

Pineapple Wassail

Snow Cocoa

Stir this cocoa all together in the slow cooker and plug in before heading out to go sledding!

2 c. WHIPPING CREAM
6 c. MILK
1 t. VANILLA EXTRACT
12-oz. PKG. WHITE CHOCOLATE CHIPS

Combine all ingredients in slow cooker. Heat on low for 2 to 2½ hours or until chocolate is melted and mixture is hot. Stir well to blend. Serves 10 chilly sledders!   ❧ KENDALL HALE ★ LYNN, MA

Creamy Nog Punch

BETTER THAN A PILE O' PRESENTS!

1 gal. vanilla ice cream
½ gal. eggnog
1 t. nutmeg
½ t. cinnamon
16-oz. container frozen
    whipped topping, thawed

*

Scoop ice cream into a punch bowl. Pour eggnog over ice cream and sprinkle with nutmeg & cinnamon; gently stir in whipped topping. Serve immediately. Stir as needed. Makes 1-½ gallons.

Creamy Nog Punch

SPICED HOT COCOA MIX

The 1st Day of Winter is December 21st...chase those flurries away with this warm mix.

1 vanilla bean
1⅓ c. sugar
1⅓ c. powdered milk
1 c. baking cocoa
3 T. instant espresso
½ t. cinnamon
¼ t. vanilla powder
⅛ t. ground cardamom

Split vanilla bean; scrape seeds and place in a medium mixing bowl, discarding shell. Add sugar; stir to blend. Add remaining ingredients; mix well. Spoon into an airtight container; attach instructions. Makes about 3½ cups.

Instructions: Stir ¼ cup mix into one cup boiling water; stir until dissolved. Makes one serving.

CHRISTMAS MORNING CAPPUCCINO MIX

Slip a jar into a stocking for an early morning treat.

⅔ c. instant coffee granules
1 c. powdered sugar
1 c. powdered non-dairy creamer
1 c. chocolate drink mix
½ c. sugar
¾ t. cinnamon
⅜ t. nutmeg
2 12-oz. jars and lids

Blend coffee granules until fine; place in a large bowl and add remaining ingredients. Stir until well mixed. Divide mixture between the 2 jars; secure lids and attach instructions. Makes 2 jars.

Instructions: Mix 3 tablespoons cappuccino mix with ¾ cup hot water or milk. Makes one serving.

Jennifer Clingan
Dayton, OH

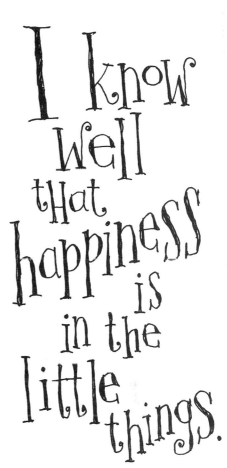

I know well that happiness is in the little things.

— JOHN RUSKIN

Apple-Cranberry Sparkler

MOM'S CRANBERRY TEA
Makes plenty for your holiday visitors.

3 6-inch cinnamon sticks
30 whole cloves
4 qts. water, divided
16-oz. can jellied cranberry sauce
2 6-oz. cans frozen orange juice
    concentrate, thawed
1 c. sugar
6 T. lemon juice

Combine cinnamon sticks, cloves and 2 cups water in a small saucepan; bring to a boil and boil for 10 minutes. In a large bowl, combine cranberry sauce, orange juice, sugar and lemon juice; add boiling liquid, straining cinnamon sticks and cloves. Pour mixture and remaining water into a slow cooker; heat on low setting to keep warm until serving. Makes about 5 quarts.

APPLE-CRANBERRY SPARKLER
Looks oh-so pretty when served In lovely holiday glasses.

4 teabags
2 c. boiling water
1 c. cranberry juice cocktail, chilled
1 c. apple juice, chilled
2 t. sugar

Place teabags in boiling water and brew for 5 minutes; remove teabags. Combine tea, juices and sugar in a pitcher and chill. Makes one quart.

Ranae Scheiderer
Beallsville, OH

"Have a holly jolly Christmas,
It's the best time of the year.
I don't know If there'll be snow,
But have a cup of cheer."
— *Johnny Marks*

sweet holiday treasures

A Christmas without sweets just wouldn't be Christmas! This assortment of cakes, pies, cookies and candy offers everything from traditional flavors to flavorful new recipes...and every morsel is just as scrumptious as the one before!

PEPPERMINT CANDY CHEESECAKE

Drizzle strawberry syrup on each slice right before serving for a merry little touch.

1 c. graham cracker crumbs
3/4 c. sugar, divided
6 T. butter, melted and divided
1 1/2 c. sour cream
2 eggs
1 T. all-purpose flour
2 t. vanilla extract
2 8-oz. pkgs. cream cheese, softened
1/4 c. peppermint candies, coarsely crushed
Garnish: frozen whipped topping, thawed; crushed peppermint candies

Blend crumbs, 1/4 c. sugar and 1/4 cup melted butter in bottom of ungreased 8" round springform pan; press evenly over bottom. Blend sour cream, remaining sugar, eggs, flour and vanilla in a blender or food processor until smooth, stopping to scrape sides. Add cream cheese and blend; stir in remaining 2 tablespoons melted butter until completely smooth. Fold in crushed candy and pour over crust. Bake at 325 degrees for 45 minutes. Remove from oven and run a knife around edge of pan. Cool, then refrigerate overnight. Loosen pan sides and remove springform; serve garnished with whipped topping and crushed candy. Makes 12 servings.

Bobbi Carney
Centennial, CO

Peppermint Candy Cheesecake

COOKIES & CREAM CAKE

For even more chocolatey taste, try using chocolate sandwich cookies with chocolate filling...yum!

18¹/₂-oz. pkg. white cake mix
1¹/₄ c. water
¹/₃ c. oil
1 t. vanilla extract
3 eggs
1 c. chocolate sandwich cookies, crushed

Combine cake mix, water, oil, vanilla and eggs in a large mixing bowl; blend on low speed until just moistened. Blend on high for 2 minutes; gently fold in crushed cookies. Line two 8" round baking pans with wax paper; grease and flour pans. Pour mix into pans; bake at 350 degrees for 25 minutes or until a toothpick inserted in the center removes clean. Cool for 10 minutes; remove from pans to a wire rack to cool completely. Frost. Serves 12.

Frosting:
¹/₂ c. butter or shortening
1 t. vanilla extract
4 c. powdered sugar
¹/₄ c. milk

Beat together butter and vanilla until creamy. Add powdered sugar and milk alternately to creamed mixture, beating until desired consistency.

Shari Miller
Hobart, IN

Dip pretzel rods in melted chocolate, then coat with chopped nuts and crushed peppermint candies...arrange in a holiday glass filled with coarse sugar for a stand-up treat.

Cookies & Cream Cake

SOFT GINGERBREAD COOKIES

My mother always made these cookies at Christmastime when I was a little girl. I carried on the tradition for my children and now make them for my grandson. They are so soft and moist...a true favorite.

1 c. margarine
1¹/₂ c. brown sugar, packed
2 eggs, beaten
1 T. ground ginger
¹/₂ c. molasses
1¹/₂ c. boiling water
1¹/₂ t. baking soda
5 c. all-purpose flour
2 t. baking powder
1¹/₂ t. salt
1 T. cinnamon
1 c. chopped walnuts

Cream margarine and sugar in a large mixing bowl; blend in eggs. Mix in ginger and molasses; stir in boiling water. Set aside. Combine remaining ingredients except for the nuts; add to sugar mixture. Fold in walnuts; cover and refrigerate dough for at least 2 hours. Drop by teaspoonfuls onto ungreased baking sheets; bake at 425 degrees for 10 to 12 minutes. Makes about 6 dozen.

Bev Johnstone
Delaware, OH

Merry Munchers!

...My daughter's favorite cookie! This recipe can easily be doubled...perfect for holiday cookie exchanges and parties.

½ c. butter
1 c. sugar
½ c. brown sugar, packed
3 eggs
1 c. creamy peanut butter
1 t. vanilla extract
1 T. baking soda

4½ c. quick-cooking oats, uncooked
½ c. semi-sweet chocolate chips
½ c. candy-coated chocolates
1 c. chopped nuts

Cream butter & sugars in a large bowl until fluffy. Add eggs, peanut butter, vanilla & baking soda, beating well. Stir in remaining ingredients and mix well. Spoon onto greased baking sheets; bake at 350 degrees for 12 to 15 minutes. Makes 25 cookies.

~Janie Branstetter ★ Fairview, OK~

Merry Munchers

PUMPKIN PRALINE LAYER CAKE

I think this is the type of dessert that's so delicious, it makes your toes curl up!

1 c. brown sugar, packed
½ c. butter
¼ c. whipping cream
¾ c. chopped pecans
2 c. all-purpose flour
2 t. pumpkin pie spice
1 t. baking soda
1 t. salt
1⅔ c. sugar
1 c. oil
4 eggs
2 c. canned pumpkin
1¾ c. whipping cream
¼ c. powdered sugar
¼ t. vanilla extract
Garnish: pumpkin pie spice and toasted chopped pecans

Combine first 3 ingredients in a heavy saucepan over low heat until brown sugar dissolves; stir occasionally. Divide equally between 2 greased 9" round cake pans. Sprinkle evenly with pecans; let mixture cool slightly. Sift together flour, baking powder, spice, baking soda and salt in a bowl; set aside. Blend sugar, oil and eggs; alternately add pumpkin and reserved dry ingredients. Spoon batter evenly over pecan mixture in cake pans. Place pans on a baking sheet and bake at 350 degrees for 35 to 45 minutes or until centers test clean. Cool cakes in pans on a wire rack for 5 minutes; invert and cool completely on wire rack. Beat whipping cream until soft peaks form; stir in powdered sugar and vanilla. Continue beating until stiff peaks form. To assemble cake, place one layer on a serving plate, praline-side up; spread with whipped topping. Add second layer, praline-side up, and top with remaining whipped topping. Garnish with spice and pecans. Serves 8.

Judy Phelan
Macomb, IL

CHOCOLATE TRUFFLES

Wrap these sweets in colorful foil papers for a festive assortment.

3/4 c. butter
3/4 c. baking cocoa
14-oz. can sweetened
    condensed milk
1 T. vanilla extract
Garnish: baking cocoa, powdered
    sugar, chopped nuts, candy
    sprinkles, flaked coconut

Melt butter in heavy saucepan over low heat; add cocoa and stir until smooth. Add sweetened condensed milk; cook and stir constantly until mixture is thick, smooth and glossy, about 4 minutes. Remove from heat; stir in vanilla. Cover and refrigerate 3 to 4 hours or until firm. Shape into 1¼-inch balls; roll in desired garnish. Refrigerate again until firm, one to 2 hours. Store, covered, in refrigerator. Makes 2½ dozen.

Vickie

Chocolate Truffles

GRANDMA'S PEANUT BUTTER PIE

My grandma is a wonderful cook and baker. When we would visit, she always had a fresh-baked pie waiting.

½ c. boiling water
4 T. cornstarch, divided
3/4 c. powdered sugar
½ c. creamy peanut butter
3/4 c. sugar, divided
1 T. all-purpose flour
1/8 t. salt
3 eggs
3 c. milk
2 t. butter
2 t. vanilla extract
1/4 t. cream of tartar
9-inch deep-dish pie crust, baked

In a small saucepan, mix together boiling water and one tablespoon cornstarch. Cook and stir constantly until clear and thick; set aside to cool. In a small bowl, combine powdered sugar and peanut butter to resemble coarse crumbs; set aside. In a 2-quart saucepan, stir together ½ cup sugar, remaining cornstarch, flour and salt. Separate eggs, placing whites in a separate bowl; set aside to warm to room temperature. Add egg yolks and milk to sugar mixture; whisk until combined. Bring mixture to a boil over medium heat; cook and stir for 2 minutes. Remove from heat and stir in butter and vanilla. Sprinkle 1/3 peanut butter mixture over pie crust bottom; layer half batter over crumbs. Sprinkle another 1/3 peanut butter mix over batter and top with remaining batter; set aside. Add cornstarch

mixture and cream of tartar to egg whites; beat until soft peaks form. Gradually sprinkle remaining sugar over mix until stiff peaks form. Spread meringue over pie, being sure to touch edges of crust to seal. Sprinkle remaining 1/3 peanut butter crumbs around top edge of pie. Bake at 375 degrees for 8 to 10 minutes or until meringue is golden. Cool completely before serving. Serves 6 to 8.

Kristina Wyatt
Madera, CA

"Christmas is not a time nor a season, but a state of mind. To cherish peace and goodwill, to be plenteous in mercy, is to have the real spirit of Christmas."
— Calvin Coolidge

Peppermint Pinwheels

PEPPERMINT PINWHEELS
The prettiest cookies for the holidays!

1/2 c. shortening
1/2 c. butter, softened
1 1/4 c. sugar, divided
1 egg
1 1/2 t. almond extract
1 t. vanilla extract
2 1/2 c. all-purpose flour
1 t. salt
1/2 t. red food coloring
2 t. egg white powder
1/4 c. water
1/4 c. peppermint candy sticks,
    crushed or coarse sanding sugar

Mix together shortening, butter, one cup sugar, egg, almond and vanilla extract. Sift together flour and salt; blend into butter mixture. Divide dough in half and blend red food coloring into one half. Chill both halves until firm. Roll light dough on a lightly floured surface to form a 6"x6" square. Roll red half to same size and lay on top of light dough. Wrap in plastic wrap and chill until firm. Roll the double layer with a rolling pin to a 12"x12" square. Tightly roll up jelly-roll style; wrap in plastic wrap and chill for one hour. Slice chilled dough into 1/4-inch thick cookies. Place on ungreased baking sheets; bake at 375 degrees for 13 minutes or until lightly golden. Mix egg white powder with water; brush on warm cookies. Mix crushed candy with remaining sugar; sprinkle candy mixture or coarse sugar on top of cookies. Makes 2 to 3 dozen.

Kathy McLaren
Visalia, CA

RED VELVET CAKE
This colorful cake is a terrific choice for a holiday dessert buffet.

1/2 c. shortening
1 1/2 c. sugar
2 eggs
2-oz. bottle red food coloring
2 t. baking cocoa
1 t. salt
2 1/2 c. all-purpose flour
1 t. vanilla extract
1 c. buttermilk
1 t. baking soda
1 t. vinegar

Cream together shortening, sugar and eggs. In a separate bowl, mix together food coloring and cocoa; add to creamed mixture. Add salt, flour, vanilla and buttermilk. Alternately add baking soda and vinegar until just blended. Pour batter into 2 greased and floured 8" round baking pans. Bake at 350 degrees for 30 minutes. Cool. Spread frosting on layers and stack to form a 2-layer cake. Serves 6-8.

Frosting:
3 T. all-purpose flour
1 c. milk
1 c. sugar
1 c. shortening
1 t. vanilla extract

Combine flour and milk in a saucepan; cook over medium heat until thick. Cool. Cream together sugar, shortening and vanilla until fluffy; add to flour mixture. Beat until light and fluffy.

Stephani Hobert
Huber Heights, OH

Use a white paint pen to draw simple snowflakes or stars away from the rim on the side of a large blue mug. Let the paint dry, then fill the mug with candy. A perfect quick gift for a snacker!

ROCKY ROAD FUDGE BROWNIES

"DELICIOUS WARM... MY HUSBAND HAS TO EAT AT LEAST 2 AS SOON AS THEY COME OUT OF THE OVEN!"

1 c. BUTTER, SOFTENED
3/4 c. BAKING COCOA
1/4 c. OIL
4 EGGS
2 c. SUGAR
1 1/3 c. ALL-PURPOSE FLOUR
1/2 t. SALT
1/2 c. HOT FUDGE

TOPPING:
1 c. CHOPPED PECANS
1 c. BUTTERSCOTCH CHIPS
2 c. MINI MARSHMALLOWS
Combine & mix well.

Combine first 3 ingredients in small saucepan; heat 'til melted and smooth, stirring often. Remove from heat; set aside. Blend eggs in large mixing bowl 'til light and fluffy; mix in cocoa mixture and next 3 ingredients. Spread in a greased 13"x9" baking pan; bake at 350 degrees 'til brownies pull away from sides of pan ~ about 25 minutes. Sprinkle topping evenly on top and drizzle with hot fudge sauce. Continue baking 5 minutes; cool. Cut into bars to serve. Makes 15.

~ Rita Miller ★ Wirtz, VA

Rocky Road Fudge Brownies

ORANGE POUND CAKE

I wanted to share this old Southern recipe that our family has been enjoying for over 35 years. We just love it!

1 1/2 c. butter, softened
3 c. sugar
5 eggs
3 1/2 c. all-purpose flour
1 t. cream of tartar
1 1/2 t. baking powder
1/4 t. salt
1/2 c. milk
1/2 c. plus 5 T. orange juice, divided
1 t. vanilla extract
1 t. almond extract
4 T. orange zest, divided
1 1/2 c. powdered sugar

Cream butter; gradually add sugar, mixing until light and fluffy. Add eggs, one at a time, blending after each addition. Combine flour, cream of tartar, baking powder and salt; add to creamed mixture alternately with the milk and 1/2 cup plus 2 tablespoons orange juice, beginning and ending with flour mixture. Mix until just blended; stir in extracts and 2 tablespoons orange zest. Pour into a greased and floured 10" Bundt® pan; bake at 325 degrees for about one hour and 25 minutes. Cool. Combine powdered sugar, remaining orange zest and enough remaining orange juice to make a desired consistency to pour over cooled cake. Serves 12.

Juanita McLane
Wilmington, DE

ENGLISH TOFFEE

Sprinkle with coarsely chopped red & white peppermints or toffee chips for an extra-special delight.

1 c. butter
1¹⁄₃ c. sugar
1 T. light corn syrup
3 T. water
2¹⁄₂ c. finely chopped slivered almonds, toasted and divided
3 1.55-oz. milk chocolate candy bars, divided

Line a 13"x9" baking pan with aluminum foil. Butter foil; set aside. Combine first 4 ingredients in a 4-qt. heavy saucepan. Cook over medium-low heat, until mixture comes to a boil. Wash down crystals from sides of pan with a small brush dipped in hot water. Cook until mixture reaches the hard-crack stage or 300 degrees on a candy thermometer, stirring occasionally to prevent scorching. Remove from heat and stir in 1¹⁄₂ cups almonds. Spread candy in prepared pan; cool completely (about 30 minutes). Break 1¹⁄₂ chocolate bars in pieces and place in a small glass bowl. Microwave at HIGH 50 seconds; stir until candy melts. Spread melted chocolate over toffee mixture; sprinkle with ¹⁄₂ cup almonds. Let cool until set (about one hour). Lift foil and candy from pan. Place a 15"x10" jellyroll pan over candy and invert candy onto jellyroll pan; remove foil. Melt remaining chocolate bars as above. Spread melted chocolate over toffee; sprinkle with remaining almonds. Chill, uncovered, 30 minutes or until firm; break into pieces. Makes about 2 pounds.

Rochelle Sundholm
Creswell, OR

AMISH SUGAR COOKIES

During my 3 daughters' elementary school years, these cookies were served at all class events. I would get a thrill out of watching the parents send their kids up to the cookie counter for yet another one…not for the kids, but for themselves!

2 c. sugar
1 c. shortening
3 eggs
1 c. sour cream
1 t. vanilla extract
5 t. baking powder
5 c. all-purpose flour
1¹⁄₂ t. baking soda

Cream sugar, shortening and eggs; add sour cream and vanilla. Gradually blend in remaining ingredients; mix well. Cover and refrigerate overnight. Drop by teaspoonfuls onto ungreased baking sheets; flatten slightly with the bottom of a sugar-coated glass. Bake at 350 degrees for 9 to 11 minutes; cool completely on wire racks. Frost. Makes about 4 dozen.

Frosting:
5 T. sugar
2 T. water
3 c. powdered sugar
²⁄₃ c. shortening
1 t. vanilla extract

Add sugar and water to a small saucepan; bring to a boil. Stir and boil until sugar dissolves; remove from heat. Pour into a medium mixing bowl; set aside to cool to lukewarm. Blend in powdered sugar; mix well. Add shortening and vanilla, blending until smooth and creamy.

Patty Vance
Paulding, OH

Handy Candy Temperatures
(Temperatures are Fahrenheit)

230°-233° = thread stage
234°-243° = soft ball stage
244°-249° = firm ball stage
250°-269° = hard ball stage
270°-289° = soft crack stage
290°-310° = hard crack stage

English Toffee

Chocolate Pecan Pie

CHOCOLATE PECAN PIE

A winning combination...ooey, gooey pecan pie and chocolate!

8 sqs. semi-sweet baking
   chocolate, divided
2 T. butter
9-inch pie crust
3 eggs, beaten
¼ c. brown sugar, packed
1 c. corn syrup
1 t. vanilla extract
1½ c. pecan halves

Coarsely chop 4 squares of chocolate and set aside. In a small bowl, microwave remaining chocolate and butter together on high for one minute or until chocolate begins to melt. Whisk until chocolate mixture is smooth. Brush bottom of pie crust with a small amount of beaten egg; set aside. Stir sugar, corn syrup, remaining eggs and vanilla into a large bowl; whisk in chocolate mixture. Add nuts and chopped chocolate. Pour into pie crust and bake at 350 degrees for 40 minutes. Cool on wire rack. Serves 8.

Debi DeVore
Dover, OH

WALNUT CRUNCH PUMPKIN PIE

This brings back special memories of evenings spent shelling nuts with my mother. What a good time we would have...the jokes and laughter flew faster than the nutshells!

16-oz. can pumpkin
12-oz. can evaporated milk
2 eggs
¾ c. brown sugar, packed
1½ t. cinnamon
½ t. salt
½ t. ground ginger
½ t. nutmeg
9-inch pie crust
Garnish: frozen whipped topping,
   thawed

Sprinkle snowflake-shaped glitter onto a clear glass plate, then top with another clear glass plate to hold glitter in place...so sweet for serving cookies!

Blend first 8 ingredients in a large bowl with hand mixer at medium speed until well mixed. Place pie plate with crust on oven rack; pour in pumpkin mixture. Bake at 400 degrees 40 minutes or until a knife inserted one inch from the edge comes out clean. Cool; sprinkle walnut topping evenly over pie. Change oven to broiler setting. Place pie 5 to 7 inches below broiler and broil about 3 minutes or until topping is golden and sugar dissolved. Cool on wire rack; garnish with whipped topping. Makes 10 servings.

Walnut Topping:
1 c. chopped walnuts
¾ c. brown sugar, packed
4 T. butter, melted

Mix ingredients well in a small bowl.

Judy Voster
Neenah, WI

INSTRUCTIONS

FAMILY CALENDAR
(shown on page 9)
Spend memory-making family time together creating this scrapbook-type calendar, then share a photocopy version of it with grandparents or other family members! Use our example here for a December idea, then just use assorted scrapbooking supplies and photos befitting to the season to complete pages for the rest of the year.

- assorted colors and textures of cardstock, including 2 full 8½"x11" sheets for the calendar backgrounds
- photographs (original or photocopied)
- hole punch
- ribbon
- self-adhesive photo mounts
- decorative-edge craft scissors
- 3 silver scrapbooking tags with seasonal wording
- scrapbooking paper-fasteners
- craft glue stick
- letter to Santa (original or photocopied)
- dimensional foam dots
- alphabet, numeral and Christmas icon stamps and inkpads
- 1½" diameter circle punch
- 5/16" diameter round letter tags for days of week
- small jute
- three 1" diameter loose-leaf rings

To decorate the top page of the calendar, cut out a cardstock tag large enough to accommodate each photo to be used. Punch a hole in each tag and knot a length of ribbon through each hole; use photo mounts to attach photos to the tags. Use craft scissors to cut rectangle strips to accommodate

2 of the silver tags; use paper fasteners to attach the silver tags to the strips. Glue the letter to a piece of cardstock, then tear the cardstock larger on each side than the letter. Arrange the letter and tags on one of the background sheets. Use glue and foam dots to attach the elements to the page.

For the bottom calendar page, photocopy the calendar layout, page 138, onto the remaining background sheet. Glue a length of ribbon across the top of the page. Stamp "December" onto cardstock; use craft scissors to cut out a rectangle around the month word. Glue the month to another piece of cardstock, then cut out a rectangle around the month piece; glue to the top of the page. Use the circle punch to cut 7 circles from cardstock. Glue one round letter tag to each circle and poke a hole in the circle through the hole in the letter tag; knotting on the backside, tie short lengths of jute through the holes in each letter tag and circle. Use foam dots to attach the circles and paper fasteners to attach the remaining silver tag to the calendar page.

Stamp the dates of the month onto cardstock; cut out a rectangle or square around each date; glue the dates to the calendar. For the holiday "stickers," stamp an icon onto cardstock, then cut out the cardstock just outside the stamped lines. Use foam dots to attach the icons to the calendar. Aligning holes, punch 3 holes along the bottom of the top calendar piece and 3 holes along the top of the bottom piece; use rings to connect the calendar pieces.

FAMILY PHOTO TREE
(shown on page 10)
The tree is the theme for this time of year, so why not make your tree really personal and unique...your family tree that is? Let the memory makers in your life shape the branches of this special tree.

Discard the glass and remove the back from a wooden picture frame; cover the back with decorative paper. Cut a piece of cardstock ¾" smaller on each side than the frame opening; cut a piece of decorative paper ½" smaller on each side than the cardstock piece. Center the paper piece on the cardstock piece (this is the mat); sew along the mat edges.

Place the mat on a flat surface centered under the frame opening. Arrange, then trim your photos to stack into a tree shape within the frame opening. Adhere each photo to cardstock; use decorative-edge craft scissors to trim the cardstock just larger than the photo. Arrange and glue the photos on the mat. Arrange a length of ¼" wide ribbon 1½" longer than each row of photos below the photos. Attach ribbon lengths to the mat with paper fasteners. Center and adhere the mat to the frame back.

For the nameplate, use paper fasteners to attach a label holder, large enough to accommodate tiles spelling out the family name, to cardstock, then cut the cardstock into a rectangle just larger than the label holder. Cut a rectangle larger than the nameplate from corrugated cardboard; glue it on the mat for the tree trunk. Center and glue the nameplate to the trunk.

Cut a star from yellow foam; glue to the tree for the topper. For each ornament, poke a tiny paper fastener through the top of a purchased scrapbook-size ornament; spread prongs on the backside. Coil one end of a 2" length of 24-gauge wire; wrap the remaining end around the paper fastener on the backside of the ornament. Hang the ornament by the coil from one of the ribbons on the tree…if you can't find pre-made ornaments, make your own by cutting ornament shapes from foam, then gluing decorative paper to each side.

CARD OR PHOTO ORGANIZER
(shown on page 11)
Hummm? Where'd I put that card I just got — or Mary Elizabeth's picture with Santa? Well, never wonder again…the answers will be right at your fingertips with this handy holiday organizer.

Use decorative paper to cover the lid of a white photo storage box gift-wrap style. Glue jumbo rick-rack along the inside bottom edge of the lid; adhere coordinating border stickers (or a strip of vellum) along the edges of the lid. Overlapping, trimming and piecing as necessary, cover the sides of the box with vellum.

For the label on the end of the box, adhere the desired word sticker to cardstock. With the word centered in the opening of a label holder large enough to accommodate the word, draw around the holder on the cardstock; cut out the cardstock just inside the drawn lines. Glue the label holder to the cardstock piece, then glue the cardstock piece to the box.

Select a photograph to go on the lid. Glue the photo to cardstock, then trim the cardstock larger on each side than the photo; attach a small paper fastener to each corner of the photo. Glue the matted photo to 2 more layers of cardstock, trimming or tearing each layer just a bit larger than the previous one. Use photo mounts to attach the matted photo to the lid.

Embellish the lid of the box with glued-on snowflake or word charms, spiraled paper clips and stamped tags. To make the tile letter tags, stamp all but the first letter of the desired word onto cardstock; leaving room for a tile letter, tear the word out and glue it to another piece of cardstock. Glue a tile letter to the tag. Arrange, then glue or use double-sided self-adhesive foam dots to attach the tags to the lid.

KID-MADE CARDS
(shown on page 12)
Let this holiday season be Christmas as seen through the eyes of a child. Hand the kids or grandkids a pack of crayons, markers or watercolors and a piece of cardstock and let them draw and color their favorite thoughts of Christmas…be sure they add their signature and the year to the artwork (or you can add a typed nameplate).

When their masterpiece is complete, trim it to the desired size and glue it to a piece of cardstock; trim the cardstock to fit around the drawing. Trim, layer and stack the artwork as desired, then glue it to the front of a blank card or a piece of folded cardstock. Now, add foam or sticker embellishments, or other scrapbooking accessories and elements to each card. To make dimensional embellishments, simply use a dimensional foam dot to attach cut out cardstock motifs or purchased embellishments to the card. To make quick & easy gift package embellishments, cut out squares from foam sheets and wrap one or more squares with narrow decorative ribbon.

CHRISTMAS JOURNAL
(shown on page 13)
• mat board
• assorted cardstock
• craft glue
• patterned vellum
• spray adhesive
• small bell
• 10" length of ribbon
• dimensional foam dots
• 2" tall letters to spell "joy"
• 1/8" diameter hole punch
• six 4-hole buttons
• embroidery floss

1. From mat board, cut two 1 1/2"x6" pieces for hinges and two 6"x9" pieces for covers.

2. To cover the front, cut an 8"x12" piece from cardstock the color you want the hinge to be. Glue one hinge piece and one cover piece, 1/16" apart, to the center on the wrong side of the cardstock. Mitering corners, wrap excess paper to back of hinge and cover pieces (inside of cover) and glue to secure in place. Cut an 8"x10" piece each from vellum and cardstock; use spray adhesive to adhere the pieces together. Centering one 8" edge of paper pieces along spacing between hinge and cover and mitering corners, wrap excess paper to inside of cover and glue in place. Repeat step to cover back cover.

3. For the inside cover liners, cut two 5¾"x8¾" pieces from cardstock. Glue one of the liners inside the front cover. For the bookmark, tie the bell to one end of the ribbon. Gluing the end of the bookmark between the liner and the back cover along the top about 1" from the right edge, glue the remaining liner piece inside the back cover.

4. To decorate the front of the journal, cut a 3"x6" tag and a 2½"x5½" tag from cardstock; center and glue the tags together, then arrange and glue them on the front cover. Use foam dots to attach the letters on the tag.

5. For each blank page, cut a 5¾"x10¼" piece from cardstock. Refer to **Fig. 1** to make a hole placement template. Punch holes in the covers and blank pages.

Fig. 1

6. Stack the blank pages (or pages you may have already finished) between the covers and align the holes. For each set of holes, place a button on the front cover and one on the back cover; knotting floss on the back, use 6 strands of floss to sew the buttons together through the holes.

MEMORY SHADOW BOX
(shown on page 14)
Gather a collection of those memory-jogging tidbits and trinkets from Christmases past and display them in a timeless shadow box sure to please even Santa himself!

Begin with a wooden shadow box, new or recycled, and paint it to match your Christmastime décor. Next, cut or tear pieces from fabrics (maybe from Granny's favorite apron — but not while she's wearing it!) to fit on the back of each section of the box; glue them in place. Layer small swatches of homespun fabrics or strips of braids or twill tape here & there on the background. Now, stamp and cut out holiday sayings, verses or dates from vellum papers; glue them in the shadow box. Lastly, fill the shelves with your treasures...add pictures, buttons, wooden blocks from yesteryears, chunky wooden cut outs, labels, stamped tags or anything you want to use. If you don't have much of a collection yet, use the abundance of scrapbooking supplies and embellishments available to help you start a brand-new collection.

MEMORY WREATH
(shown on page 15)
This wreath is as simple and easy to make as cherished memories are to leave an impression in your heart.

Begin with an 18" evergreen wreath; ours is artificial, but one created from fresh pine boughs and greenery would surely add the perfect aroma to your room. Gently wrap ribbon around the wreath...use more than one kind and if it overlaps a little bit, it's okay. Select and frame a photograph of your loved one and maybe find a small scarf or hankie belonging to them as well. Shape the hankie into a background for the photo to nestle on...wire or glue the hankie, then the photo, to the wreath. Use vintage glass ornaments, buttons and jewelry pieces to fill in empty areas on the wreath. Make a wire hanger on the back of the wreath and you are ready to share your memories with your family & guests.

LATCH-HOOKED RUG
(shown on pages 16 and 17)
• 28" square of rug canvas
• clear tape
• 30" square of cardboard
• permanent markers
• drawing compass
• rotary cutter and cutting mat
• 1¼ yards red fleece
• ¾ yards white fleece
• 1 yard light green fleece
• ¼ yard green fleece
• ¾ yards dark green fleece
• ¼ yard brown fleece
• latch hook
• non-skid backing material (optional)

Read Latch Hooking, page 135, before beginning project. Finished rug is 24" square.

1. Press each edge of the canvas 2" to the wrong side. Working on the right side, use markers to draw a 4" wide border along the edges of the canvas; draw seventeen 2" diameter circles (and a few half circles) randomly on the borders.

2. Enlarge the tree pattern, page 139, by 200% on a photocopier. Transfer the pattern to the center of the canvas.

3. Use the rotary cutter and mat to cut the fleece into $3/4$" wide lengthwise strips. (If cut selvage to selvage, the strips will stretch.) Cut each white strip into $4\frac{1}{2}$" lengths; cut remaining long fleece strips into 4" long lengths.

4. Referring to the photo for color placement, hook the fleece strips into the canvas…when hooking the tree, just scatter strips of green in here & there with the dark green.

5. Follow manufacturer's instructions to apply non-skid backing material to the back of the rug, if desired.

LATCH-HOOKED WREATH
(shown on page 16)
• 30" square of rug canvas
• string, thumbtack and a pencil
• $2\frac{3}{4}$ yards red fleece
• $3/4$ yard white fleece
• $1/4$ yard green fleece
• latch hook
• hot glue gun
• 24" square of mat board
• staple gun and staples
• 18-gauge floral wire
• wire cutters

Read Latch Hooking, page 135, before beginning project. Finished wreath is 24" in diameter.

1. Refer to *Making a Fabric Circle*, page 134, to mark cutting line on canvas. Insert thumbtack through string 14" from pencil to mark the outside cutting line. Insert tack 5" from the pencil to mark the inner circle. Cut out canvas along the outer cutting line.

2. Mark a 2" wide border around the canvas piece. Draw 2" diameter circles randomly around the wreath between the border and inner circle.

3. Use the rotary cutter and mat to cut the red and white fleece into $3/4$" wide lengthwise strips. (If cut selvage to selvage, the strips will stretch.) Cut the red strips into 4" lengths; cut the white felt into 5" lengths. Filling in between the inner circle and outer border, hook the wreath red and the circles white.

4. For the backing, cut a 23" diameter circle from mat board; cut a $10\frac{1}{2}$" diameter circle at the center of the backing. Glue the wreath to the backing; wrap the outer canvas border to the back of the backing and staple in place. Cutting from edge to edge, cut the inner circle in the wreath like a pie to make 6 wedge-shapes; wrap each wedge to the back of the backing and staple in place.

5. For the bow, cutting selvage to selvage, cut one 5" wide strip from green fleece. Matching long edges, fold the strip in half, then using a $1/4$" seam allowance and leaving a 3" opening at the center, sew the

long edges together; sew the ends together at an angle. Turn the strip right-side out through the opening and sew the opening closed. Leaving about 4" long streamers, tie the bow strip into a bow with 4 loops.

6. For the knot cover, cut one 5" square from green fleece. Press the fleece square in half, then unfold; fold the edges in to the pressed line, then refold along the pressed line and tack the fold together. Thread the center of 20" length of floral wire through the knot cover; wrap the knot cover around the knot in the bow and twist the wire together to hold the cover taut. Spacing evenly between the outer edge of the wreath and the inner circle, poke a hole through the top of the wreath. Thread the wire ends on the knot cover through the hole and twist the wires together to secure the bow snuggly on the wreath. Shape the wire ends into a hanging loop, then twist the ends together to secure.

7. Cut four 5" lengths of wire; bend each length in half. With the V in the wire against the knot of the bow, glue the wire on the inside of one loop to help shape the loop. Apply one length of wire to each loop. Cut four $1/2$"x5" strips from green fleece. Glue a fleece strip over each wire length. Shape the loops.

123

NINE POINT TREE SKIRT

(shown on page 20)

- 1¼ yards red Christmas fabric
- ⅞ yard green Christmas fabric
- 9 vintage 12"x12" handkerchiefs
- 3 yards fusible interfacing
- 6½ yards ⅜"w ribbon
- assorted buttons
- 2½ yards jumbo red rick-rack
- fusible web
- fabric glue
- pinking shears
- cardboard for template

Match right sides and use a ½" seam allowance for all sewing unless otherwise indicated.

1. Cut 12" squares of fusible interfacing and iron onto the backs of the hankies.

2. Referring to Fig. 1, draw a triangle template onto cardboard and cut out. Using template, draw 9 triangles onto red fabric; cut out.

Fig. 1

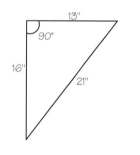

3. Referring to Figs. 2-4 for the basic placement of pieces, lay one triangle piece right side down on top of another triangle piece. Sew triangles together as indicated; press.

Fig. 2

Fig. 3

Fig. 4

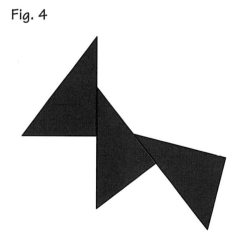

4. Referring to Fig. 5, topstitch hankies to triangles.

Fig. 5

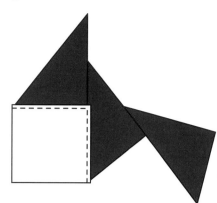

5. Cut a 27" square of green fabric. Center the tree skirt on top of fabric. Insert rick-rack between fabrics along the opening; pin together. Topstitch around opening twice for strength. Use pinking shears to trim seam allowance to 1".

6. Enlarge facing pattern, page 142, by 167%; draw pattern onto interfacing. Fuse interfacing onto wrong side of a piece of green fabric and cut out. With right sides facing, pin facing to the center of the green fabric with the tail of the facing pointing to the opening in the tree skirt. Stitch around slit and opening twice. Cut slit open and cut away excess fabric in hole. Clip seam allowance around hole to allow fabric to lay flat. Turn facing to wrong side and press.

7. Glue ribbon over the seams where hankies are joined. Glue a button to the point between hankies.

CROSS STITCHED MONOGRAM ORNAMENTS

(shown on page 25)

- embroidery floss
- 22 ct Zweigart® Antique Mushroom Hardanger
- cardboard
- striped fabric
- fleece
- felt
- ³/₈"w wire-edged ribbon
- red baby rick-rack and assorted trims
- 24-gauge wire
- assorted beads and charms
- fabric glue

Refer to Cross Stitch, page 136, before beginning project. For all sewing, match right sides and raw edges and use a ¹/₄-inch seam allowance. For each ornament, use 4 strands of floss for Cross Stitches and Backstitches and work over 2 fabric threads.

Center and cross stitch desired monogram, page 141, on cloth. For each ornament, cut a 5" square of cardboard and fleece. Glue fleece to cardboard.

For each design with circle inset, cut a 6" square of striped fabric. Cut a 3¹/₄" dia. circle from center of fabric. Turn raw edges of circle ¹/₄" to wrong side and press. Center circle over monogram and whipstitch in place. Wrap fabric square around fleece-covered cardboard. Glue raw edges of fabric to back of cardboard.

For each square design, trim stitched piece to 3¹/₂" square. Cut two 2"x6" and two 2"x3¹/₂" strips of striped fabric. Sew short strips to top and bottom of stitched piece, then long strips to sides; press. Wrap fabric around fleece-covered cardboard. Glue raw edges of fabric to back of cardboard.

For each diamond-shaped design, trim stitched piece diagonally to 3¹/₂" square. Cut two 2"x6" and two 2"x3¹/₂" strips of stripe fabric. Sew short strips to opposite sides of stitched piece and long strips to remaining sides. Wrap fabric around fleece-covered cardboard. Glue raw edges of fabric to back of cardboard.

To finish each ornament, cut an 8" piece of wire-edged ribbon for the hanger. Fold ribbon in half; glue to center back of ornament. Cut a 4¹/₂" square of felt. Glue felt to back of ornament. Embellish with beads and charms.

MONOGRAMMED PILLOW

(shown on page 26)

- 14" Graph 'N Latch® pillow cover
- 13¹/₂" square of cardboard
- white acrylic paint
- permanent marker
- red chenille yarn
- white chenille yarn
- green chenille yarn
- yarn needle
- 14" pillow form

Read Needlepoint, page 135, before beginning project.

1. Insert cardboard in pillow cover. Paint over blue grid lines with white paint. Allow to dry.

2. Using a computer, pick out your favorite font (we used CurlzMT). Print out your desired letter and enlarge to the size to fit the pillow.

3. Remove cardboard from pillow cover. Center and tape pattern to cardboard. Reinsert cardboard in pillow cover. Use permanent marker to outline pattern on canvas. Remove cardboard.

4. Referring to the photo for color placement, stitch design using 2 strands of yarn.

5. Insert pillow form.

MONOGRAMMED TISSUE BOX COVER

(shown on page 27)

Dress up your plain tissue box with a monogrammed cover created from the vintage napkin you found at the flea market. These covers are so fast & easy to make, you'll want to make more covers as gifts! Trace the desired monogram, page 141, onto tissue paper. Center the tissue paper on an oval of white fabric. Embroider monogram using 3 strands of embroidery floss for Satin Stitch and 2 strands for Backstitch. Press edges of oval ¹/₄" to the wrong side and blind stitch to a piece of white felt. Cut felt close to oval and machine stitch at center on edge of your napkin. Fold and overlap the ends of your napkin to the center. Leaving about 6" open at center for tissue, sew ends together. If your napkin isn't large enough to go around a tissue box, cut your napkin in half and add a fabric strip for an extension. Insert tissue box through one open end. With a large eye darning needle, thread 2 strands of 4mm silk ribbon through each end of napkin and tie into a bow to close. To replace tissue box, untie one end of your tissue box cover.

TABLETOP TOPIARIES AND TOMATO CAGE TREES

(shown on pages 28 and 29)
Transform ordinary wire tomato cages into whimsical Christmas trees to grace your home during the holidays.

TABLETOP TOPIARIES

- 4" dia. clay pots
- masking tape
- plaster of paris
- 9" to 12"h straight sticks for trunks
- sheet moss
- 18" square of green hand-dyed wool
- string, thumbtack, and a pencil
- black fusible interfacing
- tracing paper
- dressmaker's chalk
- pinking shears
- hot glue gun
- 4" lengths of twisted wire
- gold felt
- burgundy embroidery floss
- decorative fiber trim for garland

If you want a less full tree, use a larger seam allowance or cut off a portion of your tree body (like a slice of pie…yum…pie!).

1. For each tree, if there is a hole in the bottom of your pot, cover hole with tape. Follow manufacturer's instructions to mix, then fill pot with plaster, to within about a half-inch from top; insert stick into pot and let harden. Glue moss over plaster, covering completely.

2. For tree, cut an 18" circle from wool square following *Making a Fabric Circle, page 134*; cut along folds of wool square to make four tree bodies (set three aside for additional Tabletop Topiaries). Fuse interfacing to wrong side of wool. Trace scallop pattern, page 147, onto tracing paper; cut out. Use chalk to draw pattern along the curved edge of the interfacing, adjusting pattern as necessary and repeating the pattern as needed. Cut out.

3. Matching right sides, using a ¼" seam allowance, and leaving the top 1" unsewn, sew edges of wool together; pink seam allowance. Leaving the top 1" unturned, turn wool right side out to form tree.

4. For star topper, follow Step 9 of Single-Tier Tree (page 127) to make a star ornament. Cut a smaller star shape for backing. Glue end of wire to back of topper; glue backing star over wire. Bend wire as desired.

5. For garland, wrap trim around tree, gluing or tacking ends as necessary to secure.

6. Insert wire end of star topper into top of tree; glue to secure.

SINGLE-TIER TOMATO CAGE TREE

- large round tomato cage
- 14-gauge wire
- wire cutters
- 4" dia. wire ring (like used in macramé)
- cream felt
- green hand-dyed wool fabric
- cream, gold and burgundy felt
- fiberfill
- black, heavy-duty fusible interfacing
- dressmaker's chalk
- quilting thread for hand basting
- gold and burgundy embroidery floss
- scalloped-edge craft scissors
- pinking shears
- hot glue gun
- tracing paper
- decorative fiber trim for garland

1. For tree, turn tomato cage upside down. Gather and wrap a length of wire 3" from ends of stakes. Trim stake ends just above wrapped wire. Dab a bit of hot glue on the cut ends for safety.

2. Slide wire ring over top of tree until it fits snuggly. Cut six 36" wire lengths. Wrap one wire end around the 4" ring a couple of times, then

wrap it around each of the next cage rings (Fig. 1); trim wire end if necessary. Adding two wire lengths between each cage stake, repeat with remaining wire lengths.

Fig. 1

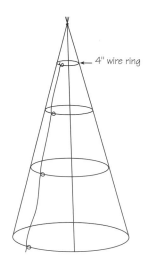

4" wire ring

3. Measure the tree height and add 3"; measure around the bottom of the tree and add 3". Cut a piece of cream felt the determined measurement. Overlapping at back and trimming as necessary to fit, wrap excess felt at bottom to inside of tree; secure with glue.

4. For base of tree, measure around the tree bottom and add 2". Use pinking shears to cut a 6"w strip of wool the determined measurement. Work a basting stitch along one long edge of strip. With basted edge 4" from bottom of tree and overlapping ends of strip at back, pull basting thread to fit strip closely to tree; tack in place. Wrap excess felt at bottom to inside of tree; glue to secure.

5. For tree tier, measure the tree height and add 1"; measure around the bottom of the tree and add 3". Use pinking shears to cut a piece of wool the determined measurement. Fuse a 4"w strip of interfacing along the bottom edge on wrong side of tier. Trace scallop pattern, page 147, onto tracing paper; cut out. With

scallops along edge of tier, use chalk to trace pattern onto interfacing repeating the pattern as necessary to fit the length of the tier; cut scallops in tier.

6. Fold the top of the tier 1" to wrong side and with one short edge even with top of tree, wrap and glue felt around tree. Leaving a small opening at top for inserting topper, glue folded edge at top of tree together.

7. For star topper, trace the star topper pattern, page 143, onto tracing paper; cut out. Using pattern, cut two stars from gold felt. With wrong sides together and using a $^3/_8$" seam allowance, sew stars together. Use scalloped-edge scissors to trim edges of topper to $^1/_4$". Cut a small slit in back of star; stuff star with fiberfill and sew opening closed.

8. For each double penny on star topper (one covers slit in back of topper), use scalloped-edge scissors to cut a $1^1/_2$" dia. circle from burgundy felt and a $2^1/_4$" dia. circle from green wool. Work gold *Straight Stitches*, page 137, along the edges of the burgundy circle; repeat with burgundy floss on the green circle. Insert a length of wire through slit in topper and glue to secure; layer and glue double pennies to front and back of topper. Insert topper into hole at top of tree.

9. For each star ornament, trace the star pattern, page 143, onto tracing paper; cut out. Draw around pattern twice on gold felt. Cut out one star just inside the drawn lines and the other star just outside the drawn lines. Work burgundy *Blanket Stitches* along the small star edges. Layer and glue to the larger star.

10. To finish tree, wrap garland trim around tree, gluing or tacking ends as necessary to secure. Glue ornaments to tree.

FOUR-TIER TOMATO CAGE TREE
- small tomato cage
- 14-gauge wire
- wire cutters
- 4" dia. wire ring (like used in macramé)
- cream felt
- green hand-dyed wool fabric
- cream, dark gold, and burgundy felt
- batting
- fiberfill
- black, heavy-duty fusible interfacing
- dressmaker's chalk
- quilting thread for hand basting
- dark gold and dark red embroidery floss
- scalloped-edge craft scissors
- pinking shears
- assorted small buttons
- hot glue gun
- tracing paper
- decorative fiber trim

1. For tree, use three 24" lengths of wire and follow Steps 1—4 of Single-Tier Tree, pages 126-127.

2. For each scalloped-edge tier, measure around tree where the bottom of your tier will fall. Cut a 9"w piece of wool the determined measurement. Fuse a 3"w strip of interfacing along one long edge on wrong side of wool piece. Trace scallop pattern, page 147, onto tracing paper; cut out. With scallops along edge of tier, use chalk to trace pattern onto interfacing and repeat the pattern as necessary to fit the length of the piece; cut scallops in tier. Work a basting stitch along remaining long edge of tier. Begin with bottom tier and work to the top. With basted edge at top and overlapping ends at back, pull basting thread to fit top of strip snuggly to felt; tack in place.

3. For treetop, cutting the fabric circle in half instead of fourths, follow Steps 2 and 3 of Tabletop Trees, page 126. Inserting wire through opening in treetop, place treetop over top of tree. Glue in place.

4. For star topper, follow Step 7 of Single-Tier tree, page 127, then work burgundy *Straight Stitches*, page 137, along the edges of the star.

5. For each heart penny for star topper (one to cover slit in back of topper), use scalloped-edge scissors to cut a 2" dia. circle from burgundy felt. Trace heart pattern, page 143, onto tracing paper; cut out. Using pattern, cut heart from wool. Work gold *Straight Stitches* along the edges of the heart, then work gold *Blanket Stitches* along the edges of the circle; sew a button to the heart. Layer and glue heart and circle to topper. Insert a length of wire through slit in topper and glue to secure; attach remaining heart penny over slit in topper.

6. For each single penny ornament, use regular scissors to cut a 1" dia. circle from burgundy felt; work gold *Blanket Stitches* along the edges. Sew a button to ornament then glue to tree.

7. For each double penny ornament, use scallop-edge scissors to cut a $1^5/_8$" dia. circle from burgundy felt and regular scissors to cut a 1" dia. circle from cream felt. Work green *Straight Stitches* along the edges of the burgundy circle and gold *Blanket Stitches* along the edges of the cream circle. Layer circles and sew a button to center. Glue ornaments to tree.

8. For each star ornament, follow Step 9 of Single-Tier Tree, page 127.

9. For garland, gluing or tacking ends to secure, wrap trim around tree. Glue star ornaments to tree over garland.

DYED WOOL AND EMBROIDERY DRAWSTRING BAG

(shown on page 31)
Compliment your holiday wardrobe with this beautifully embroidered drawstring bag or use it as a gift bag and fill it with goodies for a special friend.

For bag, cut one 16"x24" piece each of flannel and green hand-dyed wool. For border, cut one 2"x24" strip of cream felt, one 2½"x24" strip of burgundy felt, and tear one 3"x24" strip of homespun fabric. Cut out seven ⅞" dia. circles from burgundy felt and seven ⅝" dia. circles from gold felt. Use a ¼" dia. hole punch to punch seven circles from green wool, seven circles from light green felt, and 18 circles from burgundy felt. Cut seven 6" lengths of ⅛"w variegated green silk ribbon.

Refer to photo, page 31, to overlap the ends of the ribbons and tack ribbon "vines" to the cream felt strip. For large flowers, secure a green wool circle to the center of each gold circle with a *French Knot*. Work green *Blanket Stitches* to attach gold circles to ⅝" dia. burgundy circles. Work gold *Blanket Stitches* to attach flowers to border. Attach light green circles with dark green *French Knots*. Attach sets of three burgundy ¼" dia. circles with gold *French Knots*. Work *Lazy Daisy* leaves along ribbon vines.

Working gold *Blanket Stitches* along the edges, attach the cream strip to the burgundy strip. Layer strips on top of fabric strip and machine stitch 6" from top of green wool piece. Match right sides

of green wool piece and machine stitch ends together. Turn right side out. Matching wrong sides, work gold *Blanket Stitches* to join felt circle to bottom of tube.

For lining, press one long edge of flannel ½" to wrong side. Match right sides of flannel and machine stitch ends together. Do not turn right side out. With right sides together and matching raw edges, sew flannel circle to bottom of tube. Matching seams and wrong sides, slip flannel lining in felt bag. Pin along the top edge and sew together. Using seam line as a guide for the stitch length, work gold *Blanket Stitches* along top and bottom edges of bag.

For drawstring casing, machine stitch around bag 2½" from top, then 3½" from top. Clip open seam in felt at casing and insert a 36" long piece of twisted cording. Tie cording at the ends and loop together with an overhand knot.

DYED WOOL COVERED OTTOMANS

(shown on page 29)
Impress visitors to your home with a classy ottoman dressed up for the holidays. Using ottoman kits and wool felt, you can create your very own unique piece of furniture.

PENNY RUG OTTOMAN
Follow manufacturer's instructions to cut burgundy wool felt to cover ottoman. Position and pin felt to top of ottoman. Trace star pattern, page 142, onto tissue paper. Using pattern, cut four stars from gold wool felt. Pin a star to each corner of ottoman cover. For borders, tear 3" wide strips of homespun fabric to fit

between stars; pin to top between stars. Remove felt from ottoman; work *Blanket Stitches*, page 136, to attach stars and machine stitch fabric strips to felt.

For pennies, cut three 1" circles each from oatmeal, gold, and burgundy wool felt, three 2" circles each from burgundy, green and gold wool felt, and three 3" circles each from oatmeal, green and gold wool felt. For each penny, alternating colors, layer circles and work *Blanket Stitches* to attach them together. Referring to photo, arrange pennies on top of ottoman to create a diamond shape. Work *Blanket Stitches* to attach pennies to cover. Cover ottoman with decorated felt cover. Use fabric glue to add ¼" burgundy cording between ottoman sections.

TREE OTTOMAN
Follow manufacturer's instructions to cover ottoman with burgundy check homespun and to insert 1" dia. cording covered in burgundy wool felt between sections. For scalloped trim, cut a 4" wide strip of green wool felt long enough to wrap around the ottoman and overlap slightly at back. Trim one long edge of strip in a scallop pattern; work gold *Blanket Stitches* along scallops. Cover 1⅛" buttons with burgundy homespun; sew a button to every scallop. Attach skirt to ottoman below cording. Cut a square of green wool felt approximately 2" smaller than top of ottoman. Using decorative-edged scissors, cut a square of gold wool felt ½" smaller than green square. Layer squares; work burgundy *Running Stitches* along the edges to join. Cut a piece of burgundy wool felt ½" smaller than gold piece; center and work green *Blanket Stitches* to attach it to gold felt. Cut a piece of oatmeal felt wool

same width as burgundy felt and approximately 5½" high, then trim one long edge unevenly to form the snow bank. Line up snow bank with bottom of burgundy felt and work *Blanket Stitches* to sew it in place. Trace patterns, page 144, onto tissue paper. Using patterns, cut stars from gold wool felt and trees from green wool felt. Cut ornaments from oatmeal, gold, and burgundy wool felt; work *Blanket Stitches* to attach to trees. Refer to photo to work *Blanket Stitches* to attach trees and stars in place. Use green floss to stitch decorated felt to top of ottoman.

Floral Ottoman

Follow manufacturer's instructions to cover top of ottoman with green flannel fabric. For ruffle, measure around ottoman and cut an 8" wide strip of flannel twice the length of measurement. Matching right sides, sew ends of strip together. Turn one long edge ½" to wrong side and hem. Sew a gathering stitch along remaining raw edge. Pull gathering stitches until ruffle fits around ottoman. Follow manufacturer's instructions to cover bottom of ottoman with ruffle. Glue a length of twisted cording between top and bottom of ottoman. For embroidered design, cut a piece of oatmeal wool felt 1" smaller on all sides than top of ottoman. Cut lengths of green variegated ribbon; tack it in place as the stem. Trace pattern, page 142, onto tissue paper. Using pattern, cut 11 leaves from green wool felt. Work green *Running Stitches* down center of each leaf for veins. Cut 14 ¾" dia. circles from dark green wool felt, three 4" dia. circles from burgundy wool felt, and three 3¼" dia. circles from gold wool felt; layer to form flowers. Arrange flowers and leaves

along ribbon stem; work *Blanket Stitches* to attach. Attach ⅞" dia. burgundy buttons as berries. When design is complete, work *Blanket Stitches* to attach decorated piece to top of ottoman.

QUILT
(continued from page 35)
Place backing wrong side up on a flat surface. Place batting on top of backing fabric. Center quilt top right side up on batting. Begin in center and work toward outer edges to hand baste all layers together. Use long stitches and place basting lines approximately 4" apart. Smooth fullness or wrinkles toward outer edges. Machine quilt using a decorative stitch and sewing along seams.

Cut two 2½"x55" and two 2½"x68" lengthwise or crosswise strips of fabric for binding. Piece strips to achieve necessary length. Matching wrong sides and raw edges, press strips in half lengthwise to complete binding. Matching raw edges, sew a length of binding to top and bottom edges on right side of quilt. Trim backing and batting from top and bottom edges ¼" larger than quilt top. Trim ends of top and bottom binding even with edges of quilt top. Fold binding over to quilt backing and pin pressed edges in place, covering stitching line; blindstitch binding to backing. Leaving approximately 1½" of binding at each end, stitch a length of binding to each side edge of quilt. Trim backing and batting as above. Trim each end of binding ½" longer than bound edge. Fold each end of binding over to quilt backing; pin in place. Fold binding over to quilt backing and blindstitch in place, taking care not to stitch through to front of quilt.

RIBBON STAR
(shown on page 38)
For each star, cut six 4" lengths of 1½" wide ribbon and a 2" dia. circle of felt. Fold ribbon into loops, Fig. 1, and glue to secure. Evenly spacing, glue ribbon loops in place around felt circle. Cover a 2" dia. button with coordinating fabric; sew to center of felt circle covering ribbon ends. Layer a ⅜" dia. button and a ⅝" dia. button; sew to center of covered button. For hanger, cut a 10" length of ⅜" wide ribbon; tack ends to back of ornament.

Fig. 1

RIBBON CIRCLE
(shown on page 38)
Cut two 10" lengths of 1½" wide ribbon. Cut one 10" length of ⅜" ribbon; sew along center of one 10" ribbon. With right sides together, sew ends of ribbon lengths together. With wrong sides together, one side of ribbon lengths together. Work *Running Stitches*, page 137, to sew along remaining edge of one ribbon. Pull threads to gather ribbon into a circle; before tying off, stuff ornament with batting. Layer a ⅜" button and a ⅝" button; sew to center of ornament. For hanger, cut an 8" length of ribbon. Fold ribbon in half and tack fold to top center of ornament; knot ends.

BRAIDED GARLAND
(shown on page 38)
For each braid, cut 1³/₄" wide strips of fabric. Wrap a fabric strip around a length of ⁵/₁₆" dia. cording; sew next to cording with zipper foot. Cut off excess fabric with pinking shears. Braid three lengths together; sew ends together to secure.

WOVEN BASKET
(shown on page 38)
Beautify a plain, simple basket by tearing strips from your favorite fabric and weaving them through the basket splints. Use a butter knife to help weave the fabric through the splints. If needed, glue the fabric ends in place to secure.

DRAWSTRING GIFT BAG
(shown on page 39)
• green floral flannel
• green cotton fabric
• assorted ribbons
• square buttons

Match right sides and use a ¹/₂" seam allowance for all sewing.

1. Cut two pieces of flannel to the desired size for your gift bag. Cut two pieces of cotton fabric the same size for lining.

2. Lay one flannel piece on a flat surface; lay lengths of ribbon horizontally across flannel piece and pin in place. Weave additional lengths of ribbon vertically across flannel piece and pin in place. Sew ribbons in place using decorative stitches. Sew buttons along ribbons.

3. For bag, with right sides together and leaving top open, sew flannel pieces together. To form bottom corners, match side seams to bottom seam; sew across each corner 1" from end.

Fig. 1

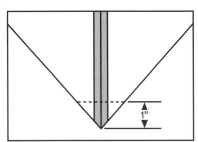

4. Repeat Step 3 for lining.

5. With right sides together, place bag inside lining. Leaving an opening for turning, stitch together along top edge,. Turn bag right side out and press. Topstitch ¹/₈" from top edges of bag to close opening.

6. To form the drawstring casing, topstitch the long edges of a length of ribbon across top back of gift bag.

7. For drawstrings, cut two lengths of ribbon approximately 2¹/₂ times the width of your gift bag. Beginning and ending on opposite sides of casing, use a safety pin to thread one drawstring through casing, woven ribbon on front, and back through casing; knot ends together. Repeat with remaining drawstring.

SNOWFLAKE TOPIARIES
(shown on page 46)
The art of topiary has been practiced for hundreds of years. Topiaries have become popular focal points for landscaping as well as for interior decorating. Try your hand at creating these snowflake topiaries as the focal point of your holiday decorating.

Begin with 3 sizes of clay pots and 3 dowel rods; working in a well-ventilated area, spray paint white. Covering drain holes in pots with tape, follow manufacturer's instructions to mix and fill pots halfway with plaster; insert dowel rods. Allow plaster to set up until firm.

Read *Working with Polymer Clay*, page 137, then follow the polymer clay manufacturer's instructions to condition clay; run clay through a pasta machine (used for clay only) on the #1 setting. Using cookie cutters, cut out snowflakes. Following the instructions on the clay package, bake snowflakes in the oven. Once cooled, spray snowflakes with spray adhesive and sprinkle with mica snow glitter. Repeat on back of snowflake.

Hot glue snowflakes to dowel rods. For largest pot, layer 2 snowflakes. Using dimensional foam dots, adhere a sticker to the center of each snowflake. Tie a length of ribbon into a bow around dowel rod.

Use double-stick tape to adhere torn strips of fabric to the rims of the pots. Stamp words on blue cardstock; insert in metal tags and tie around rims using ribbon. Fill pots to brim with chenille fabric.

ORIGAMI TREE
(shown on page 50)

- red, yellow, blue, brown, light green and green cardstock
- $1/4$" and $1/2$" dia. hole punches
- silver earring hooks
- silver jump rings
- 3"x6" foam cone
- 7" length of $1/2$" dia. dowel rod
- $3/4$" dia. circle punch
- glitter
- craft glue
- straight pins (optional)
- tracing paper

1. Cut 2" from the top of the cone. Cover the cone with brown paper; glue in place or secure with straight pins.

2. Insert 3" of the dowel into the top of the cone.

3. For bottom tree section, start with a 12"x12" piece of light green cardstock. Referring to **Figs 1-4**, fold in half diagonally four times.

Fig. 1

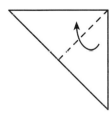

Fig. 2

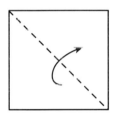

Fig. 3

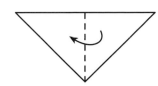

Fig. 4

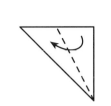

4. Referring to **Fig. 5**, cut away ends.

Fig. 5

5. Unfold tree section...refold along original fold lines, accordion style.

6. For middle tree section, repeat Steps 3-5 using a 10"x10" piece of green cardstock.

7. For top tree section, repeat Steps 3-5 using an 8"x8" piece of light green cardstock.

8. Using both hole punches, punch holes randomly along edges of each tree section. Apply glue, then glitter along edges of tree sections. Allow to dry and top off excess glitter.

9. Cut a small hole at center of each tree section. Slide dowel rod in tree base through center of each tree section. Spacing sections evenly and leaving a small section of dowel rod at top for the star, glue tree sections in place along dowel rod.

10. Punch $3/4$" dia. circles from red, yellow, light green, and blue cardstock. Punch a $1/4$" dia. hole near edge of each circle.

11. Apply swirls of glue, then glitter to half of the ornaments. Allow to dry and tap off excess glitter.

12. For hangers, insert a jump ring or an earring hook through the hole in each circle. To decorate tree, insert hangers through holes along edges of tree sections.

13. Using the pattern on page 149, follow *Making Patterns*, page 134, to trace the star pattern onto tracing paper. Using the pattern, cut two stars from yellow cardstock. Following the dotted lines on pattern, fold each star.

14. Leaving an opening along bottom, glue the points of the stars together. Apply glue, then glitter along edges of star. Allow to dry and tap off excess glitter.

15. Slip star onto top of dowel rod; glue in place.

PINWHEEL ORNAMENT
(shown on page 50)
For each ornament you will need:
• green and yellow cardstock
• 1/2" red foam heart
• 1 1/2" dia. flower punch
• 1/8" and 1/16" dia. hole punches
• mica snow
• craft glue
• scallop-edged craft scissors
• 1/4"w red ribbon

1. Using craft scissors, cut a 1 1/2"x12" strip of green cardstock.

2. Using both hole punches, punch holes along one long edge of strip.

3. Using approximately 3/8" wide folds, accordion fold strip.

4. Cut a 2" dia. circle from yellow cardstock. Bend short ends of folded green strip together to form pinwheel; glue together. Glue the center back of pinwheel to the circle.

5. Punch a flower from yellow cardstock; glue to center front of pinwheel.

6. Thin a small amount of craft glue with water; brush over center of ornament. Sprinkle mica snow glitter over glue; allow to dry, then tap off extra glitter.

7. Glue heart to center of ornament.

8. For hanger, thread ribbon through one hole punched in ornament; tie ends together.

BUTTON ORNAMENT
(shown on page 50)
For each ornament you will need:
• Christmas vellum
• red cardstock
• ceramic Christmas button
• 8" length of red trim
• craft glue
• 1/4" dia. hole punch

1. Cut two 4"x10" strips of vellum. Referring to Fig. 1, accordion fold strips, then fold down a triangle between each accordion fold. Fold each strip then glue one short end of each strip to the short end of the other strip. Fan strips into a circle to form ornament.

Fig.1

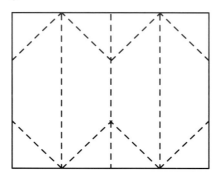

2. Cut a 1 1/2" dia. circle from red cardstock; glue to center front of ornament.

3. Glue button to center of cardstock.

4. For hanger, punch a hole along the top front of ornament; thread trim through hole; tie ends together.

BIRD ORNAMENT
(shown on page 50)
• red and yellow cardstock
• red glitter
• 1/4" dia. wiggle eyes
• 1/3 yd 1/2"w red ribbon
• 1/8" dia. hole punch
• tracing paper

Using the patterns on page 149, follow Making Patterns, page 134, to trace the patterns onto tracing paper. Using patterns, cut bird and wings from red cardstock and beak from yellow cardstock. Fold beak in half as indicated by dotted line on pattern; glue to bird. Using approximately 1/3" folds, accordion fold wings; insert through body of bird and glue in place. Glue wiggle eyes to bird's head. Thin a small amount of craft glue with water; brush over sides and wings of bird. Sprinkle glitter over glue; allow to dry, then tap off extra glitter. Punch a hole along center top of bird. For hanger, thread ribbon through hole; tie ends together.

WISH LIST ALBUM
(shown on page 52)
Children will love making this Wish List to proudly show when asked what they want for Christmas. Using the patterns on page 149, follow Making Patterns, page 134, to trace the patterns onto tracing paper. Using patterns, cut one small tag from red cardstock and several large tags from red and green corrugated paper. Stamp child's name onto small tag and embellish with a foam snowflake sticker. For hanger, tie a small length of thread through hole and tie ends together. Thread large tags and hanger of small tag onto a shower curtain ring. Use foam alphabet stickers to spell "Wish List" on first large tag. Let the child cut pictures out of a catalog of those special things that they just "have to have," then glue the pictures to the large tags.

NOTEPAD BOOKLET

(shown on page 53)
- 3" square notepad
- mat board
- scrapbook paper
- two 1/2" dia. buttons
- embroidery floss
- craft knife
- craft glue

1. Cut a 3 1/2"x7 1/2" piece of mat board.

2. Referring to Fig. 1, use craft knife to score mat board, then bend board to create folds in booklet. When folded, the short end will overlap the long end by approximately 1/2".

Fig. 1

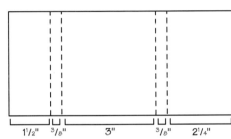

| 1 1/2" | 3/8" | 3" | 3/8" | 2 1/4" |

3. Wrapping ends to inside of booklet and securing with glue, cover booklet with paper.

4. Using 6 strands of embroidery floss and poking holes through mat board, sew buttons 1/2" from edge of short end and 1" from edge of long end of booklet. For closure, tie one end of a 10" length of floss to one of the buttons; wrap around both buttons to close booklet.

5. For inside cover, glue a 3"x7" piece of scrapbook paper to inside of booklet. Adhere notepad to inside of booklet.

SANTA DOLL

(shown on page 56)
- 1/4 yard red corduroy
- 1/8 yard white chenille fabric
- 1/8 yard white cotton fabric
- peach and black felt
- 5/8 yard 3/8" w plaid ribbon
- gold metallic thread
- white chenille yarn
- polyester fiberfill
- black embroidery floss
- fabric glue

Match right sides and use a 1/4" seam allowance for all sewing unless otherwise indicated.

Bring Santa to life with this cuddly doll. Enlarging the body pattern by 155% and following *Making Patterns,* page 134, use the patterns on pages 150-152, to trace the patterns onto tracing paper; cut out. Using patterns, cut one beard, one mustache, two hat brims and two hat tassel pieces from chenille fabric. Cut one beard and one mustache piece from white fabric for backing. Cut face from peach felt. Cut four mittens and four boots (two each in reverse) from black felt. Cut two bodies and two gussets from corduroy. Cut four arms and four legs (two each in reverse) from corduroy.

With wrong sides matching, machine satin stitch white fabric to back of beard and mustache. Work *French Knots* on face pieces for eyes.

For front of Santa, glue face piece approximately 2 1/2" from top of body front piece. Topstitch hat brim to body front along top of face. Sew one tassel to top of body (Fig. 1); press to right side. Repeat to sew beard to bottom of face. Sew mustache in place using red thread and a machine satin stitch for nose. Machine satin stitch a length of ribbon 3 1/2" from bottom of body piece for belt; machine satin stitch buckle with gold metallic thread. Using six strands of floss, work *French Knots* for buttons.

Fig. 1

For back of Santa, sew remaining tassel to top of back body piece; press to right side. Topstitch hat brim to back piece. Machine satin stitch ribbon in place for belt.

Sew one mitten to end of each arm. Leaving top of each arm open, sew arm pieces together; turn right side out. Stuff each arm with fiberfill; baste in place on body.

Sew one boot to end of each leg. Leaving top of each leg open, sew leg pieces together; turn right side out. Stuff each leg with fiberfill; sew to the straight edge of one gusset piece.

Matching right sides and leaving bottom open, sew body pieces together. Baste straight edges of gusset pieces together. Sew curved edges of gusset piece to bottom edges of body. Beginning at the center, remove enough basting threads in order to turn Santa right side out. Stuff Santa with fiberfill; sew opening closed. Glue yarn along edges of beard, mustache, hat brim, tassel, mittens, boots and bottom of body.

EMBELLISHED SWEATER

(shown on page 57)

Turn an ordinary sweater into a blooming beauty with a few little touches. Use a crewel needle to run a length of yarn along edges of sweater and cuffs. Use a crochet hook to chain stitch flower stems through sweater. For leaves, cut 4" lengths of ⁵/₈"w green ribbon. With right sides together, Fold each length of ribbon where the right sides of each end are together; pull ends through sweater and tack in place. For flower, cut a 7" dia. circle from felt. Refer to Fig. 1 and use yarn to cinch felt circle into a flower shape; knot yarn to secure. Use yarn to stitch veins and a *French Knot* on each flower petal. For center of flower, knot a length of 1"w ribbon 3 times; stitch to flower.

Fig. 1

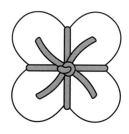

LET IT SNOW SWEATER

(shown on page 57)

When the weather outside is frightful, bundle your little one up in this delightful sweater and "Let it Snow, Let it Snow, Let it Snow." Using the snowman patterns on page 153, follow *Making Patterns*, below, to trace the patterns onto tracing paper. Using the patterns, cut the snowman from white felt, the gloves from black felt, the scarf from blue felt and the hat and nose from orange felt. Work *Straight Stitches*, page 137, to attach nose, scarf, and buttons to snowman; work *French Knots* for snowman's mouth; and work *Cross Stitches* for snowman's eyes. Work *Straight Stitches* to attach snowman to front of sweater. Add *Running Stitches* across brim of hat, then work *Straight Stitches* to attach hat and gloves to snowman. Thread alphabet beads onto a length of embroidery floss and *Couch* in place between mittens. Various sizes of white pom-pom's randomly stitched onto sweater provide the finishing touch.

SANTA POCKET ENVELOPE

(shown on page 65)

We used Christmas paper on our Envelope Gift Box but you can change the paper to fit any occasion.

Cut a 10" dia. circle from cardstock and scrapbook paper; in a well-ventilated area, use spray adhesive to adhere paper to cardstock. Score card 3" from top and bottom edges of circle then score card 3" from each side of circle. Along score marks, fold sides of circle to center. For bottom flap, fold bottom of circle up; for top flap, fold top of circle down. Cut a decorative piece of paper to fit top flap; use spray adhesive to adhere to top of flap. For closure, glue one end of a length of ribbon to back of top flap; sew a button onto bottom flap.

GENERAL INSTRUCTIONS

MAKING PATTERNS

When the entire pattern is shown, place tracing paper over the pattern and draw over lines. For a more durable pattern, use a permanent marker to draw over the pattern on stencil plastic.

When tracing a two-part pattern, draw over the first part of the pattern onto tracing paper, then match the dashed lines to trace the second part of pattern onto tracing paper.

MAKING A FABRIC CIRCLE

Matching right sides, fold fabric square in half from top to bottom and again from left to right. Tie one end of a length of string to a fabric marking pen, insert a thumbtack through string at length indicated in project instructions. Insert thumbtack through folded corner of fabric. Holding tack in place and keeping string taut, mark cutting line (Fig. 1).

Fig. 1

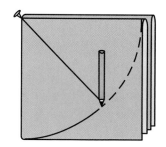

LATCH HOOKING

TRANSFERRING PATTERNS

Arrange patterns, print side up, between rug canvas and a piece of cardboard larger than the patterns; tape in place on cardboard. Use permanent marker to outline patterns on canvas. Remove canvas from cardboard.

USING THE LATCH HOOK

1. To hook strip to canvas, slide hook beneath one crossbar in canvas. Wrap one strip around hook with ends even (**Fig. 1**); slide hook back through canvas until strip is about halfway through.

Fig. 1

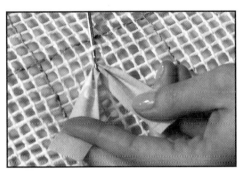

2. Leaving shaft of hook in loop, catch ends of strip in hook and pull them through the loop (**Fig. 2**). Pull knot tight (**Fig. 3**).

Fig. 2

Fig. 3

FILLING THE CANVAS

To keep canvas square, begin at one corner on the top or bottom of the canvas. Work across the row, changing strip colors as necessary, before moving to the next row. Yardages given are based on the hooking patterns below. Use this hooking pattern to ensure having enough yardage to complete the project.

Fleece diagram

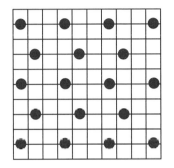

Yarn diagram

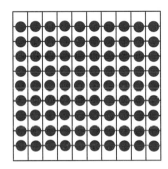

NEEDLEPOINT

STITCHING THE DESIGN

SECURING THE FIRST STITCH: Don't knot the end of your yarn before you begin stitching. Instead, begin each length of yarn by coming up from the wrong side of the canvas and leaving a 1" – 2" tail on the wrong side. Hold this tail against the canvas and work the first few stitches over the tail. When secure, clip the tail close to your stitched piece.

STITCHES: Needlepoint is worked in horizontal or vertical rows over one intersection. Stitches slant from lower left to upper right. Referring to Fig. 1, bring needle up at even numbers and down at odd numbers.

Fig. 1

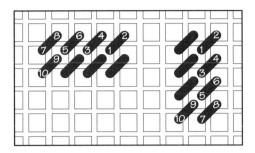

USING EVEN TENSION: Keep your stitching tension consistent, with each stitch lying flat and even on the canvas. Pulling or yanking the yarn causes the tension to be too tight, and you will be able to see through your project. Loose tension is caused by not pulling the yarn firmly enough, and the yarn will not lie flat on the canvas.

ENDING YOUR STITCHES: After you've completed all of the stitches of one color in an area, end your stitching by running your needle under several stitches on the back of the stitched piece. To keep the tails of the yarn from showing through or becoming tangled in future stitches, trim the end of the yarn close to the stitched piece.

TIPS:

- It is best to begin stitching with a piece of yarn that is approximately one yard long.
- Most stitches tend to twist the yarn. Drop your needle and let the yarn untwist every few stitches or whenever needed.

CROSS STITCH

COUNTED CROSS STITCH (X): Work one Cross Stitch to correspond to each colored square in chart. For horizontal rows, work stitches in two journeys.

Fig. 1

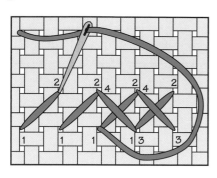

For vertical rows, complete stitch as shown.

Fig. 2

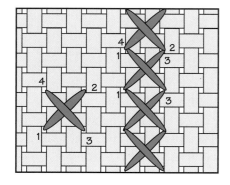

QUARTER STITCH: Quarter Stitches are shown as triangular shapes of color in chart and color key.

Fig. 3

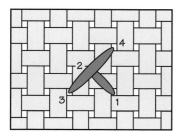

BACKSTITCH (B'ST): For outline detail Backstitch (shown in chart by black straight lines) should be worked after all Cross Stitch has been completed.

Fig. 4

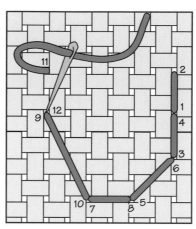

FRENCH KNOT: Referring to Fig. 5, bring needle up at 1. Wrap floss once around needle and insert needle at 2, holding end of floss with non-stitching fingers.

Fig. 5

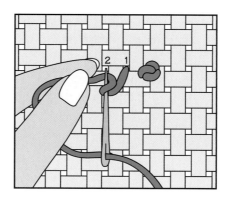

EMBROIDERY STITCHES

BLANKET STITCH: Referring to Fig. 1, bring needle up at 1. Keeping thread below point of needle, go down at 2 and come up at 3. Continue working as shown in Fig. 2.

Fig. 1

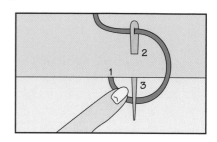

Fig. 2

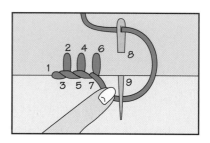

COUCHED STITCH: Referring to Fig. 3, bring needle up at 1 and go down at 2, following line to be couched. Work tiny stitches over thread to secure.

Fig. 3

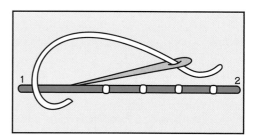

HERRINGBONE STITCH: Referring to Fig. 4, bring needle up at 1; go down at 2. Bring up at 3 and pull through; go down at 4.

Fig. 4

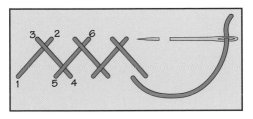

LAZY DAISY STITCH: Bring needle up at 1; take needle down again at 1 to form a loop and bring up at 2. Keeping loop below point of needle (Fig. 5), take needle down at 3 to anchor loop.

Fig. 5

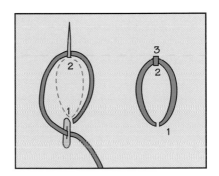

RUNNING STITCH: Referring to Fig. 6, make a series of straight stitches with stitch length equal to the space between stitches.

Fig. 6

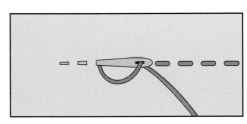

SATIN STITCH: Referring to Fig. 7, come up at odd numbers and go down at even numbers with the stitches touching but not overlapping.

Fig. 7

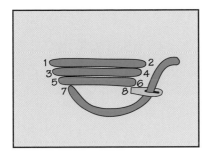

STRAIGHT STITCH: Referring to Fig. 8, come up at 1 and go down at 2.

Fig. 8

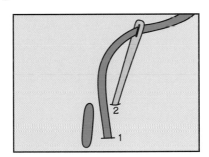

WORKING WITH POLYMER CLAY
GETTING READY
Always begin by covering your work surface. Clay should not come in contact with surfaces where food is prepared or be used on plastic or wood surfaces. Cover the surface with freezer paper, shiny side up. Tape corners of freezer paper to table or counter to hold in place while working. Designate tools used with polymer clay for use with clay only: do not use them for food preparation.

CONDITIONING
Although it may feel very soft and workable right out of the package, polymer clay should always be conditioned before use. To condition clay by hand, knead balls of clay that are a comfortable size to work with (about $1/2$ ounce) until warm and pliable.

For the projects in this book, we used a hand-crank pasta machine. This handy tool, with easy-to-adjust settings, can be used to condition clay and make clay sheets of varying thickness. To condition clay using a pasta machine, fold clay over before each pass and work out any air bubbles; simply pass clay, folded edge first, through machine set on #1 setting 10-15 times.

ROLLING CLAY SHEETS
To roll a clay sheet using a pasta machine, send conditioned clay through machine at thickest setting (#1).

BAKING
Cure clay by baking as directed by manufacturer in a standard home oven or a toaster oven designated for use with clay only. Do not use a microwave oven. Bake in a well-ventilated area. Place project on a piece of parchment paper or an index card on an aluminum pan, baking dish, or heavy-duty cookie sheet to bake.

FAMILY
CALENDAR
(page 9)

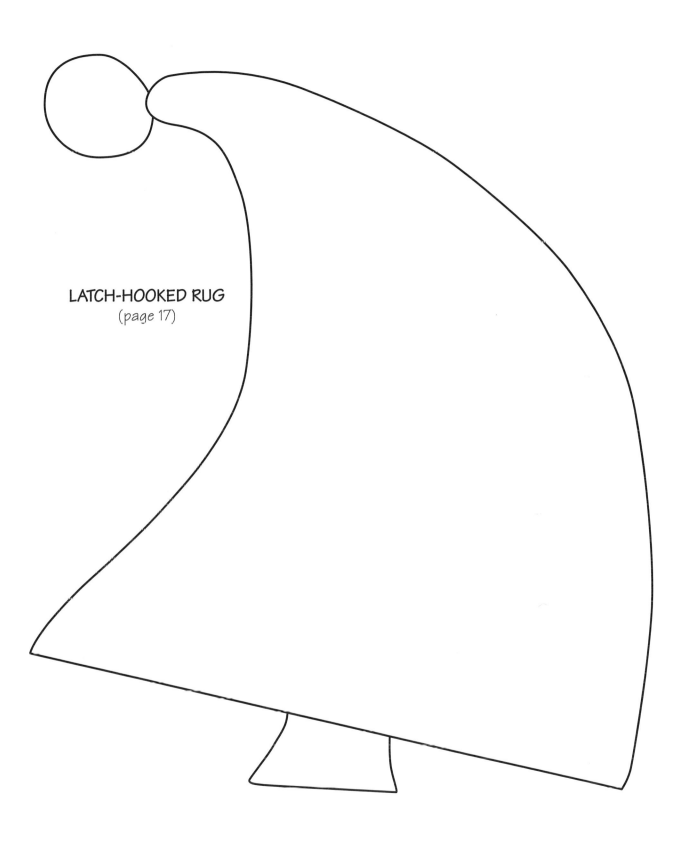

LATCH-HOOKED RUG
(page 17)

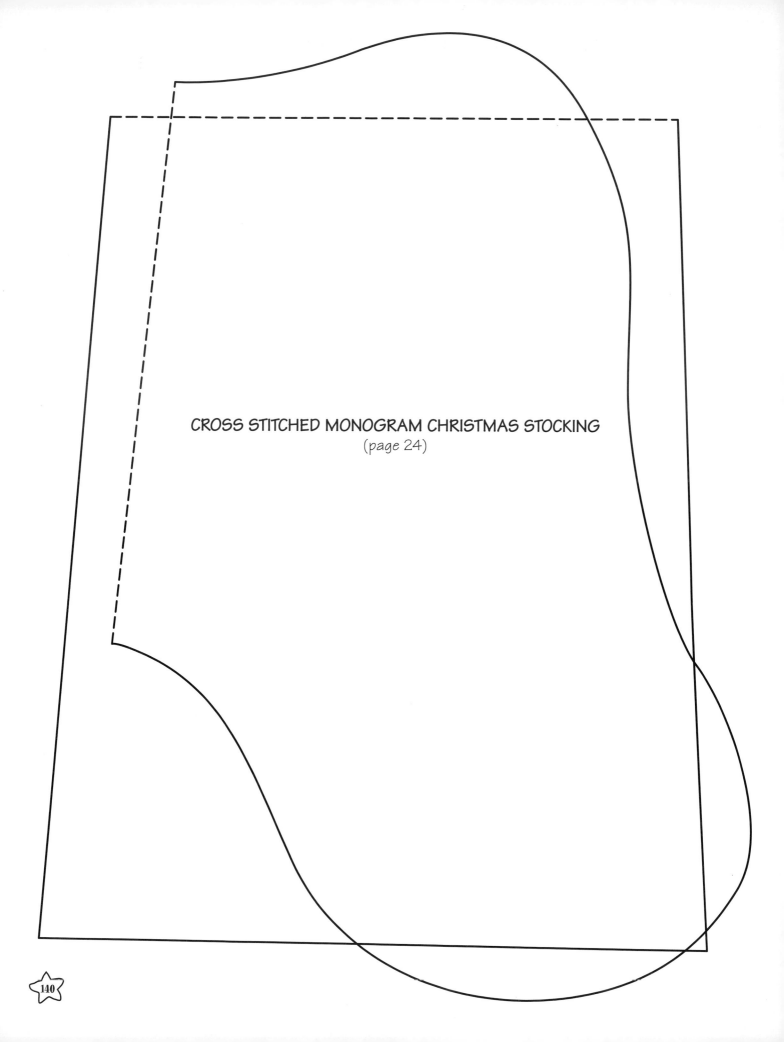

CROSS STITCHED MONOGRAM CHRISTMAS STOCKING
(page 24)

CROSS STITCHED MONOGRAM CHRISTMAS STOCKING,
CROSS STITCH MONOGRAM ORNAMENTS, MONOGRAMMED HAND TOWEL AND
MONOGRAMMED TISSUE BOX COVER

(pages 24-27)

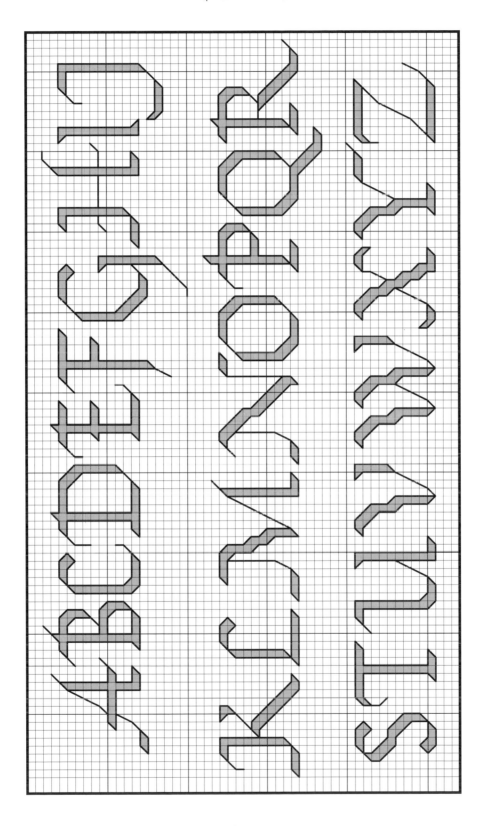

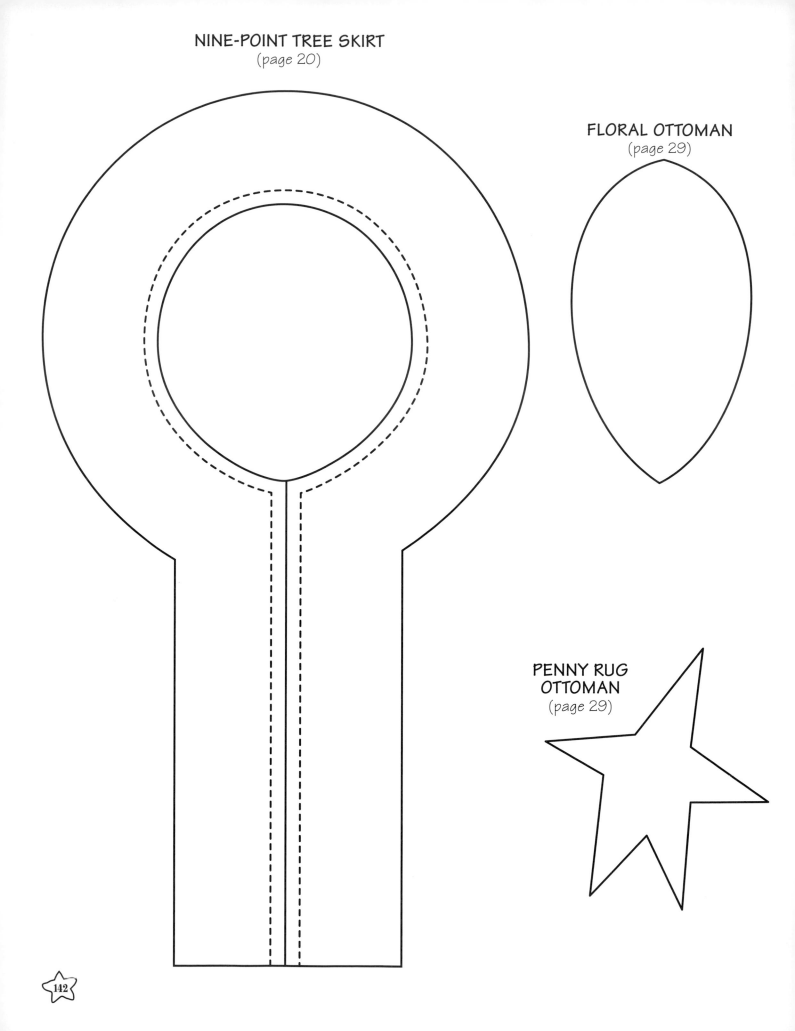

NINE-POINT TREE SKIRT
(page 20)

FLORAL OTTOMAN
(page 29)

PENNY RUG OTTOMAN
(page 29)

142

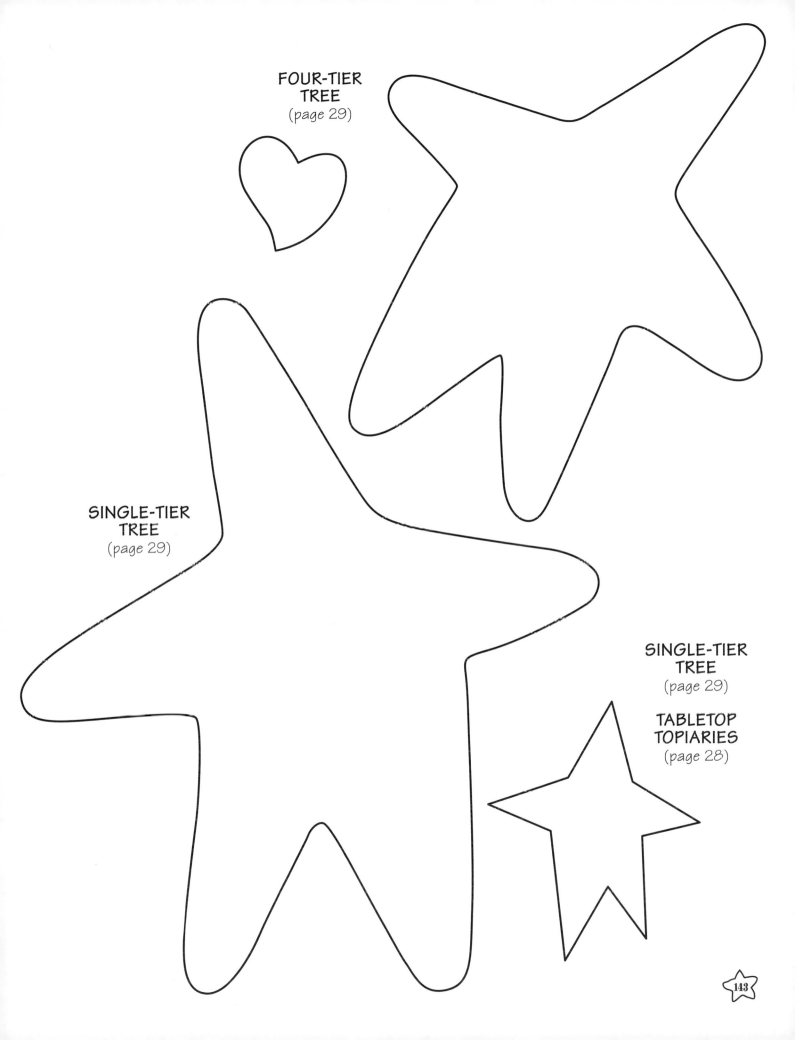

FOUR-TIER
TREE
(page 29)

SINGLE-TIER
TREE
(page 29)

SINGLE-TIER
TREE
(page 29)

TABLETOP
TOPIARIES
(page 28)

TREE OTTOMAN
(page 29)

EMBROIDERED TOTE BAG
(page 31)

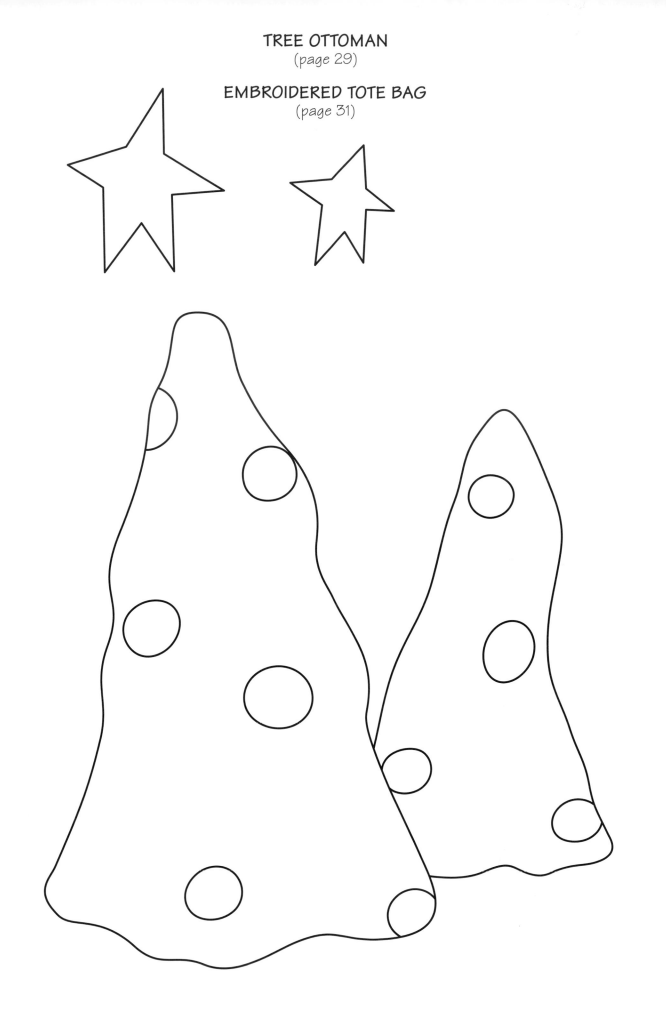

Every gift though it be small, is in reality great if given with Affection

Liddie Fudim

FLANNEL BAGS
(pages 38 and 39)

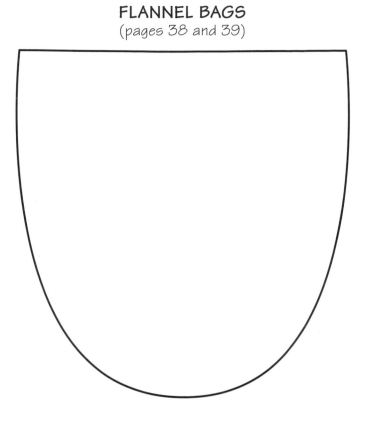

ROUND BOX ORNAMENTS
AND GIFT BOXES
(pages 43 and 48)

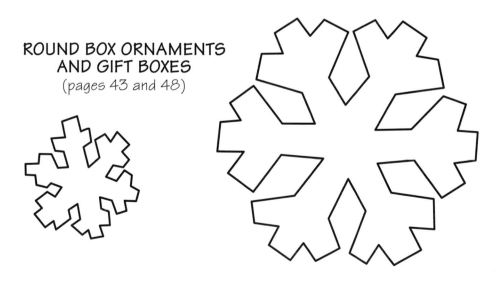

ICICLE GARLAND
(page 43)

SNOWFLAKE AND MITTEN WALL HANGING
(page 47)

TABLETOP TOPIARIES AND TOMATO CAGE TREES
(pages 28 and 29)

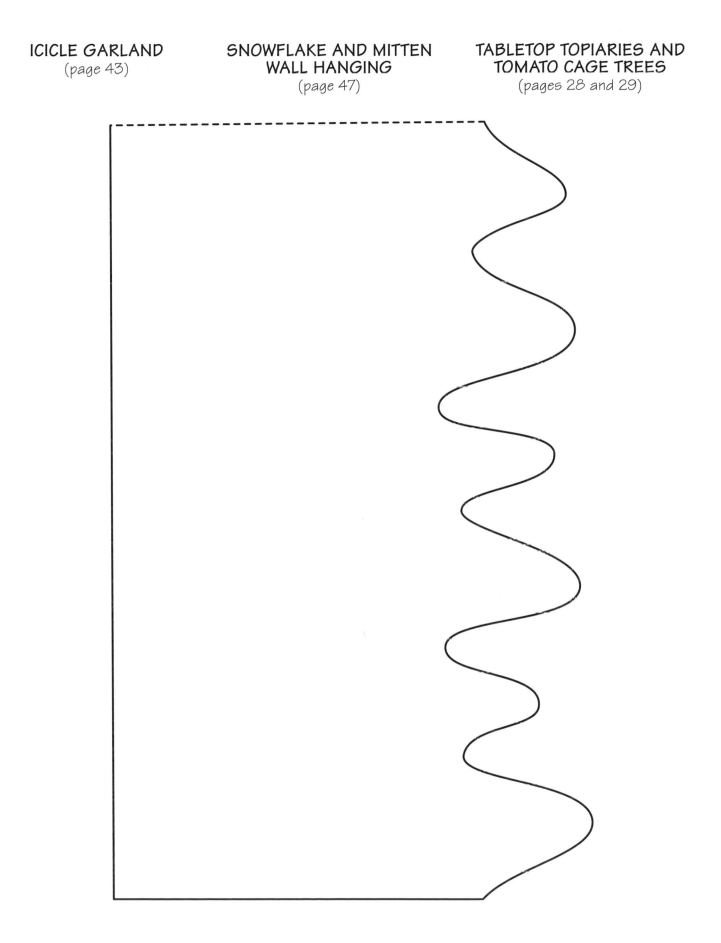

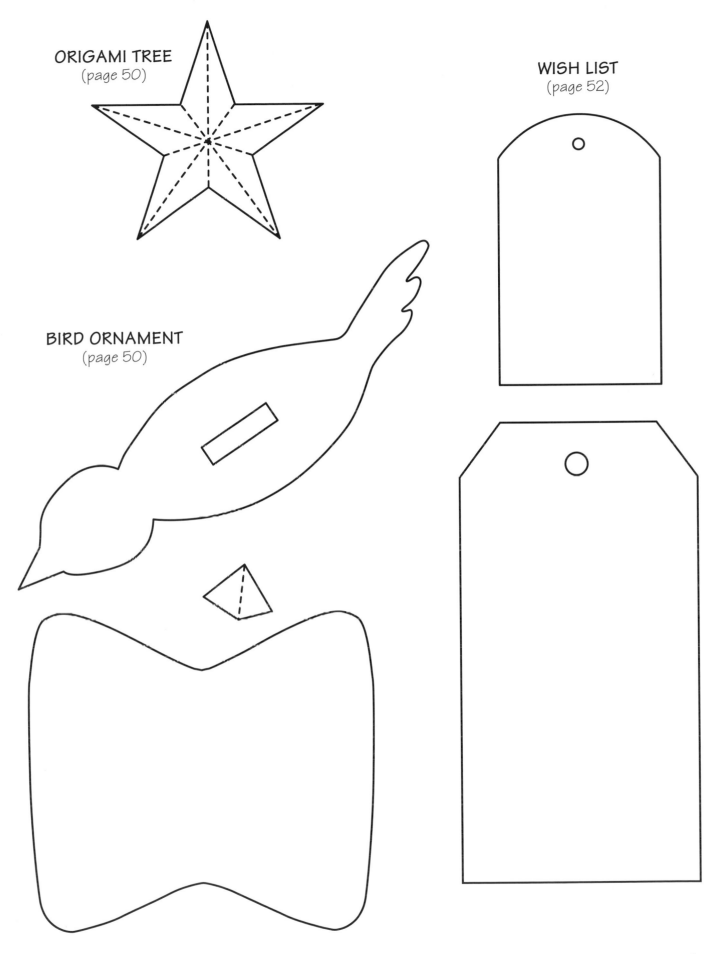

ORIGAMI TREE
(page 50)

WISH LIST
(page 52)

BIRD ORNAMENT
(page 50)

149

SANTA DOLL
(pages 55 and 56)

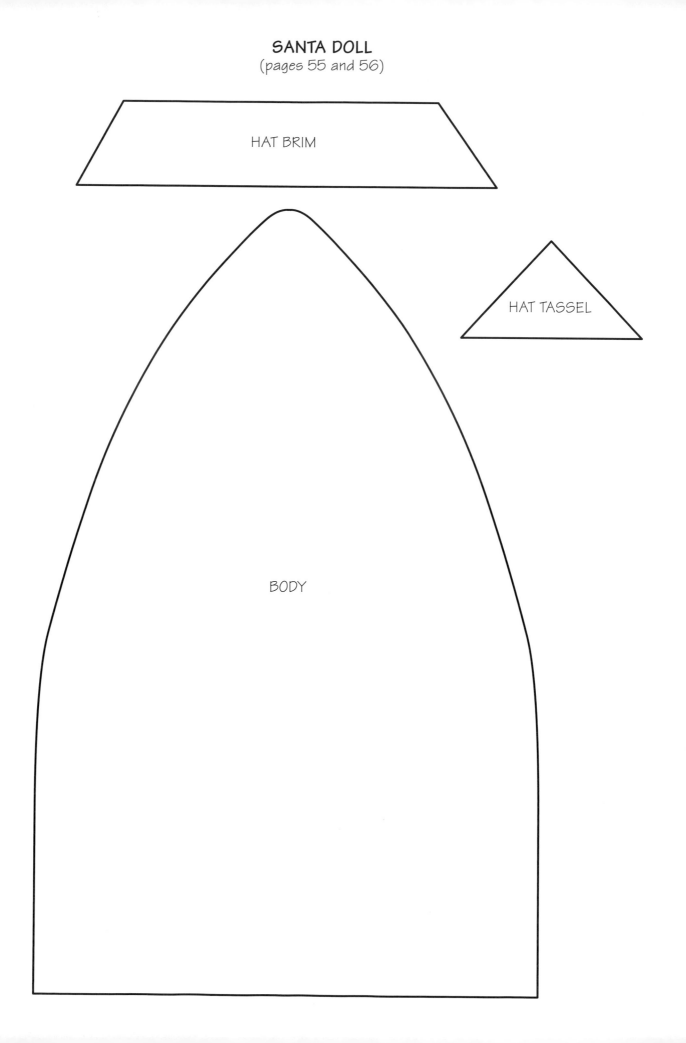

HAT BRIM

HAT TASSEL

BODY

SANTA DOLL
(page 56)

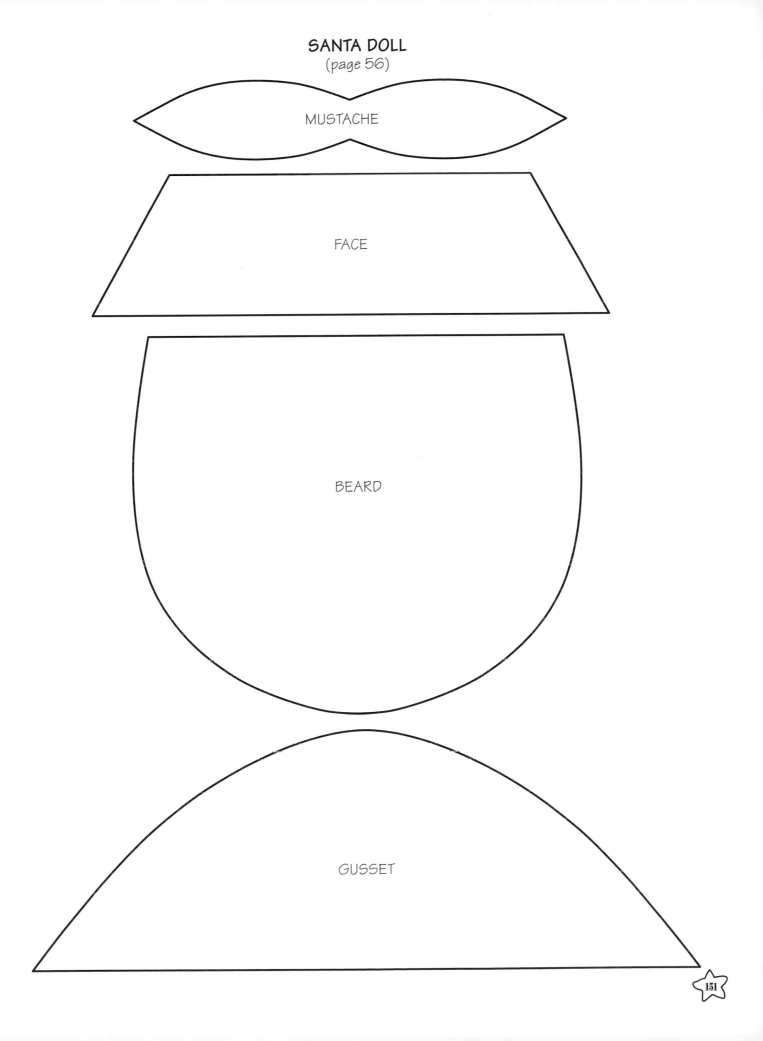

MUSTACHE

FACE

BEARD

GUSSET

SANTA DOLL
(pages 55 and 56)

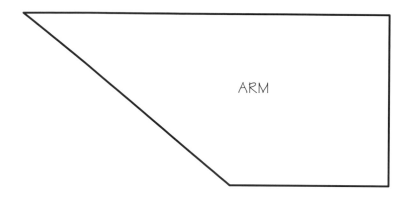

ARM

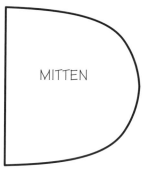

MITTEN

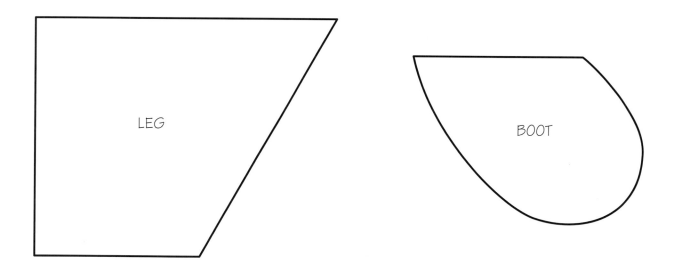

LEG

BOOT

EMBELLISHED SWEATER
(page 57)

EMBELLISHED GLOVES
(page 58)

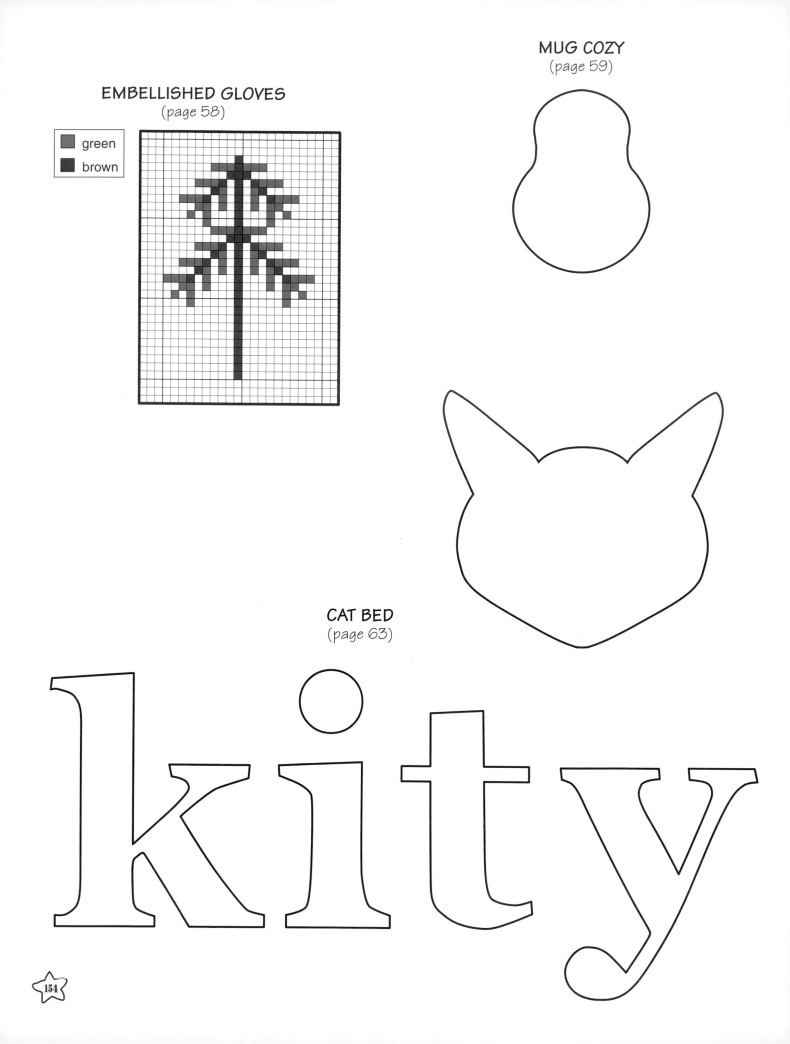

green
brown

MUG COZY
(page 59)

CAT BED
(page 63)

kity

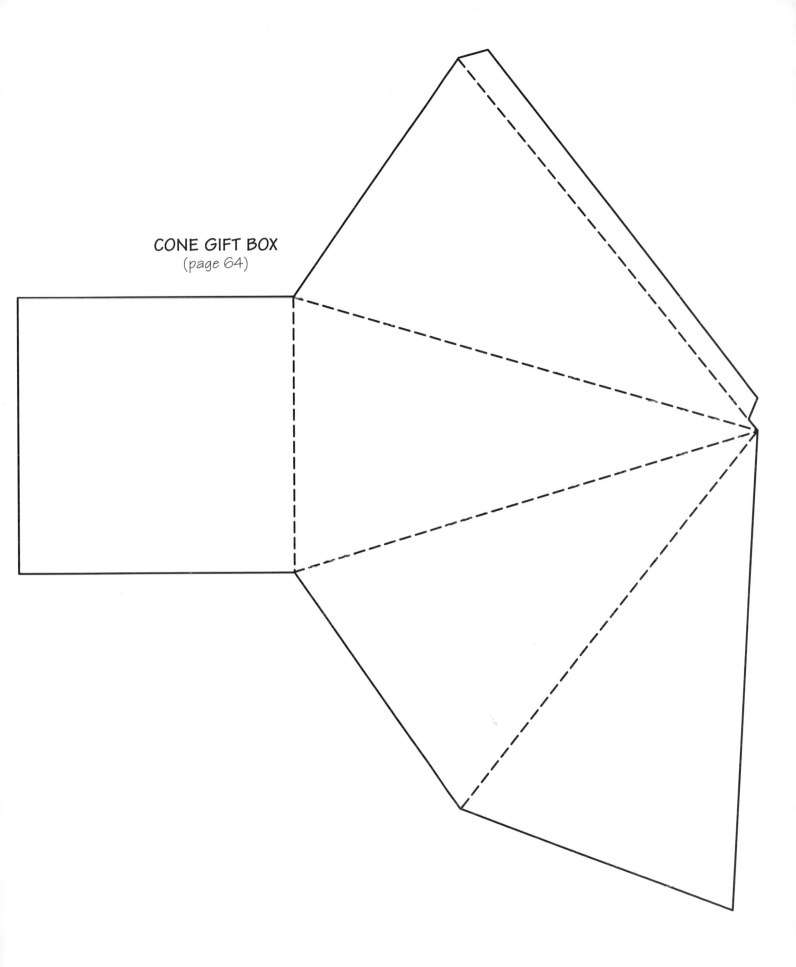

CONE GIFT BOX
(page 64)

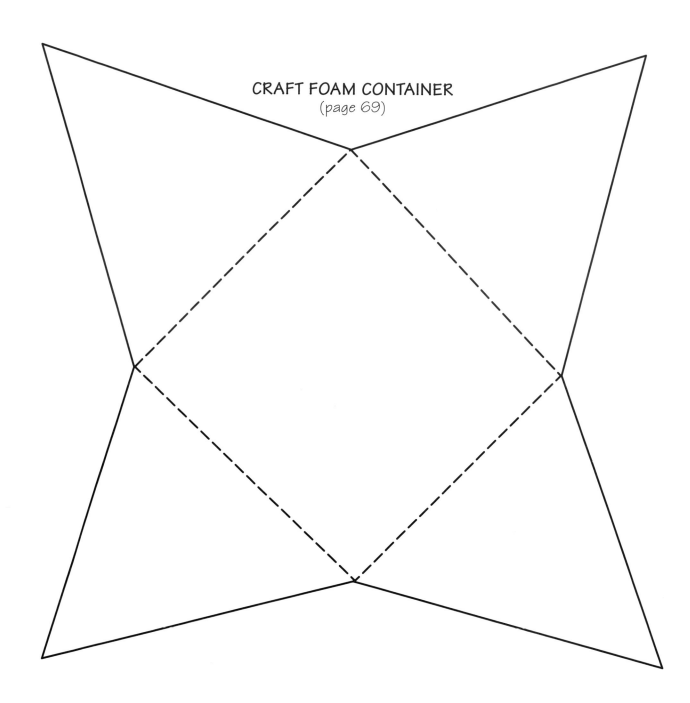

CRAFT FOAM CONTAINER
(page 69)

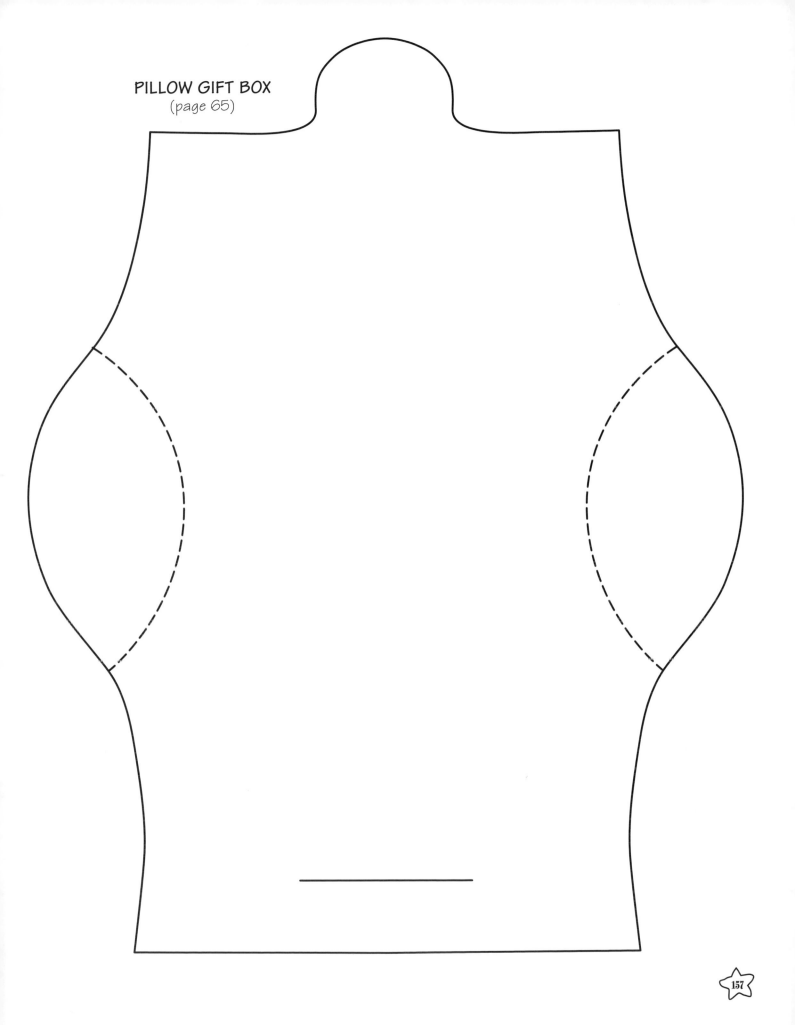

PILLOW GIFT BOX
(page 65)

PROJECT INDEX

RECIPE INDEX